The *Call*
to
ADOPTION
Becoming Your Child's Family

Jaymie Stuart Wolfe

auline
BOOKS & MEDIA
Boston

Library of Congress Cataloging-in-Publication Data

Wolfe, Jaymie Stuart.

  The call to adoption : becoming your child's family / Jaymie Stuart Wolfe.
    p. cm.

  ISBN 0-8198-1573-X (pbk.)

  1. Adoption—Religious aspects—Christianity. 2. Adoption—Psychological aspects. I. Title.

  HV875.26.W64 2005

  248.8'45—dc22

2004023195

The Scripture quotations contained herein are from the *New Revised Standard Version Bible: Catholic Edition,* copyright © 1989, 1993, Division of Christian Education of the National Council of the Churches of Christ in the United States of America. Used by permission. All rights reserved.

Excerpts from *Book of Blessings* additional blessings for use in the dioceses of the United States. Copyright © 1988, United States Conference of Catholic Bishops, Washington, D.C. Used with permission. All rights reserved. No part of this work may be reproduced or transmitted in any form without permission in writing from the copyright holder.

Photos: Michael Albarelli: p. 44; Gladys Alvarez-Fonts: p. 232; Christine Bjerke: p. 239; Bjornstrom Family: p. 178; Erik Bjornstrom: p. 168; Sabrina Bjornstrom: p. 52; Corinne Carmony: p. 98; Ginny Courtney: front cover—bottom, left; Tom and Sue Gardiula: p. 16; Rob Hess: p. 82; Kathleen A. Ravey: p. 134, 220; Sean Peck: p. 4; Jaymie Stuart Wolfe: pp. 26, 150; T. Tomasi: pp. 34, 60, 72, 114, 126, 192; Ralph Verrilli: front cover—top and middle, left, right.

"P" and PAULINE are registered trademarks of the Daughters of St. Paul

Copyright © 2005, Jaymie Stuart Wolfe

Published by Pauline Books & Media, 50 Saint Paul's Avenue, Boston, MA 02130-3491. Printed in U.S.A.

www.pauline.org

Pauline Books & Media is the publishing house of the Daughters of St. Paul, an international congregation of women religious serving the Church with the communications media.

1 2 3 4 5 6 7 8 9   11 10 09 08 07 06 05

This book is dedicated to

the Holy Family—
mystical, biological, and adoptive—

one in the unity of love and self-gift.

May the example of their life together bring
each one of us home to heaven,

as sons and daughters of our Eternal Father.

Contents

Acknowledgments

There are many people who contribute to the writing of a book, some seen and others not. I am grateful first and foremost to my husband Andrew, and to my mother. You did everything in your power to support me from beginning to end. I know how often you picked up where I slacked off. Without you, I would not be able to do anything I get credit for doing. As far as I am concerned, you deserve equal billing.

Our children feed the writer in me. Without Jana, Nadja, Kolbe, Katerina, Kyril, Austin, Juliana, and Marjeta, I would have nothing worth writing about. You have given me more than you know. In being your mother, I have learned more about life than I will ever be able to teach you. But I'll keep trying anyway.

Our family is complete because of the work of Doris and Gwyn Slaton at Bless This Child in Oklahoma. We have never met in person, but you responded to our family's vision with generosity, enthusiasm, and the expertise of your experience. You held our hand through every twist and turn.

The Call to Adoption was not my bright idea. Sister Madonna, thank you for asking me to write it, and for believing in the project even when I struggled to complete it. I cannot imagine working with a more gracious publisher than Pauline Books & Media. The faith of the Daughters of St. Paul permeates every aspect of their work.

Behind every good book is an even better editor. Diane Lynch is the best cheerleader anyone could ever have. When I wondered or worried out loud, you just cheered louder. You appreciated my challenges, and brought out the very best of my abilities.

I thank the Holy Spirit for carrying me through this work, and for leading me, in 1983, to the Roman Catholic Church. In the Bride of Christ I have found a Holy Mother, and many good priests who have fathered the faith in me. Together, we are the household of God our Father.

Introduction

For all who are led by the Spirit of God are
children of God. For you did not receive a
spirit of slavery to fall back into fear, but you
have received a spirit of adoption. When we
cry, "Abba! Father!" it is that very Spirit bearing witness with our spirit that we are children
of God, and if children, then heirs ... of God
and joint heirs with Christ....

— Romans 8:14–16

In the Spring of 2002, my husband Andrew and
I boarded a plane to Moscow, and then an overnight
train to the city of Voronezh in southern Russia. Two
days later, a Russian judge declared that a child we had
met only three weeks before was our daughter. We didn't
know much of her language. We knew even less about
her past. We did know, however, that we loved her, and
that this love made us one another's. This book is the
story of that journey, and a reflection on that love.

"Our Father, who art in heaven...." The words slip so easily past our lips, with so little hesitation, that there is not nearly enough time to consider what it is we are actually saying. On a hillside overlooking the Sea of Galilee, Jesus answered his eager disciples when they asked him how to pray. He taught them to begin by claiming God—the Eternal, Almighty Creator of all—as their father.

In that moment, Jesus gave us his Father as our own. He initiated a whole thread of teaching about the relationship God has established with us through him that, in turn, establishes our relationships with one another. But because only Jesus himself was *born* the Son of God, the rest of us must come to understand our identity as God's children in a different way. In essence, we are God's children by *adoption.* God is our Father by choice, both his and ours. We might as well pray, "Our *(adoptive)* Father."

St. Paul tells us that the Spirit of God, the Holy Spirit, is the power behind our identity as children and heirs of God. We are chosen, saved, loved, incorporated—even sealed (a legal term)—by the Holy Spirit, which then witnesses to us the truth of who we have become. That Spirit enables us to cry out to God as Father. It is not a spirit of slavery or fear, but a *Spirit of adoption.*

When we celebrate Christmas, we rejoice in the birth of the baby Jesus. We tend to overlook, however, that the Holy Family is both "natural" and adoptive. Mary gave birth to Jesus, and Joseph adopted him. Taking Mary into his house, Joseph raised Jesus "as his own." But more, in doing so, Joseph made Jesus truly his own. Joseph's life models the divine and mysterious fatherhood of God. He is not just a caregiver, but a father to the Word-made-flesh. His relationship to the child Jesus is not merely functional. It involves his identity, the core of who he is. Later on, the people of Nazareth asked, "Isn't this the son of Joseph?" The answer may not be simple, but it cannot be, "No."

The Church is also an adoptive family. Each of us approaches the baptismal font as a person created by God, and leaves it as a new creation, a son or daughter adopted by God into the family of the Church, a member of his eternal household. In Christ, people of every race and culture, and every age, otherwise unrelated to each other, are made brothers and sisters. The love of Christ challenges us to love one another well, to accept one another as part of the same family, to forgive and heal and care for each other, and to bear one another's burdens.

All of this is to say that our Christian faith gives us, from its very beginnings, a rich source for reflecting on what adoption is and what it means. It is from our self-understanding as adopted children of God that we can begin to understand what kind of love it is that leads us to adopt a child ourselves, and what kind of love it takes to sustain us in being adoptive parents. The Holy Spirit must be in our lives what he is for our souls: the life-giving fountain of grace and wisdom, our advocate, comforter, teacher, our guide and the giver of all gifts. Even more, we must experience God's Spirit as his power in us and among us moving to transform and sanctify.

The Call to Adoption is not written to promote adoption per se. My purpose here is twofold: to share our own family's joyful journey; and to encourage those who, like our family, are finding themselves walking a rather dimly lit road paved with many choices. I have no intention of pushing any particular agenda, for while almost all adoptive families consider themselves blessed, I do not believe that adoption, as wonderful as it is, is appropriate for everyone. I do, however, know the distinct call adoption had—and continues to have—in our family's life.

Because adoption doesn't just fall out of the sky, because every action that is taken flows from extended reflection and discernment, I have begun each chapter with a personal anecdote and then moved to a reflection that is both practical and spiritual. It is my prayer that any who do travel this path will experience the deeply spiritual nature of what they are doing, and find in *The Call to Adoption* a way of connecting themselves to the God whose love reaches far beyond himself to each one of us. This God we are privileged to call "Father."

1

Overflowing Love
Moved by Gratitude

What shall I return to the Lord, for all his boun-
ty to me?

— Psalm 116:12

$\mathcal{T}$he summer before our youngest child turned
two, my husband Andrew and I started wondering if
she should remain our youngest child. We dared not
tell anyone what we were thinking. With seven kids, we
were already at the far edge of the societal galaxy. Crazy
perhaps, but even though raising seven children is a
very full plate, something about it felt oddly incomplete.
We just weren't done, and we knew it.

Our first thought was to return to the familiar, and
simply have another baby. Knowing there wasn't much
tick left in the old biological clock, we didn't have the
luxury of taking a lot of time to think about it. While I

felt quite positive about having an eighth child, the thought of going through yet another pregnancy and childbirth was completely unappealing. Although I could imagine every aspect of maternity, labor, and delivery, somehow I couldn't imagine doing it all again. We began to think that perhaps we should just accept what we had and quit while we were ahead—at least in numbers—of practically everybody else we knew.

In all our considerations, one thing was indisputable. Andrew and I had been more than blessed with a wonderful family. The longer we thought about it, the more we were able to see that God had withheld nothing from us. Our children were bright, energetic, healthy, interesting, funny, and—though neither one of us is sure how this happened—attractive. While we didn't always experience it this way, our home was a hothouse of divine blessing!

It was only when we asked ourselves what we could do with all our blessings that the idea of adopting a child began to dawn on us. My husband and I began to see that what we had spent twenty years of our lives building was perhaps not just for "us." We had already expanded our daily experience of family by having both my mother and grandmother live with us. We wondered if perhaps we could stretch our concept of family even further, beyond the biological, to include a child who needed what we had to offer. Again, we were drawn forward.

As soon as adoption became a topic of discussion, our awareness of children in need grew exponentially. Andrew and I heard reports of infant girls being abandoned in other countries simply because they were girls, and stories of mothers pressured to give up their children because they could not adequately provide for them. The sheer number of orphans around the world was shocking, and the conditions they lived in even more so.

Realizing just how rich we were in love led us to consider taking the path toward adoption. As we took stock of all that we could give, we also began to see what an adopted child could give to us. Bringing a child into our family through adoption would be a way to practice the works of mercy not just on special occasions, but every day. Inviting a child who had nothing into our home, and our lives, presented a marvelous—if daunting—opportunity to live our faith. We began to understand that adopting a child was something we could give to God in gratitude for all that the Lord had done for us.

There is, I think, a basic human awareness that except for the grace of God, we would all have nothing. But as we grow in faith, we begin to understand that through that same grace we are called and empowered to lovingly respond to others in need. We have all helped a neighbor, or a sick relative, or a friend. We have all pitched in to make the world a better place in some small—or not so small—way. Grateful for what we

have, we express that gratitude by caring for and about those who have less than we do. We do so because we know that we have been blessed. We want to pass the blessing on.

Charity is love flowing in two directions. It takes a receptive giver and a generous receiver to find meaning in one another's loving actions. Adopting a child out of charity is not an unusual motivation. The challenge is to recognize that our motivations may not be as pure as we think, or hope, they are. Often, they are mixed. In retrospect, I can see that some of what moved me to adopt a child was a bit tainted. I say "tainted" because perfect love is self-*less*. It does not take the self into account, not even the self's aspiration to be holy. Love always looks to the good of the other, and because of that, neither pride nor pity has much to contribute to genuine charity.

We may start with pity for children who have no homes, but if this remains the prime motivation for adoption, the child we adopt will never become a full and equal member of his or her own family. Feeling sorry for someone interferes with our ability to love her. Actions rooted in guilt tend to bind rather than liberate; and bondage is not the same as bonding. If we overextend ourselves and try to give more than we are capable of giving, we create webs of interpersonal indebtedness. Resentment can find a home in the heart of the person who acts from a sense of doing good without fully weighing the cost. Every parent drinks from the cup of self-sacrifice. But when I've reached the dregs, I sometimes wonder whether I've allowed myself to become a bit too dependent on free refills!

Pride is another hindrance. Knowing the plight of orphaned children, many families who adopt wish that others would also consider adoption. But if we begin to applaud ourselves for doing something good, or allow others to do so, we may be exchanging true charity for something that is more directed toward *ourselves* than it is toward *others*. More than a few people have told us that we are saints for adopting a child. I'll admit that it is all too tempting to take the bait and secretly agree with them. While I wish becoming holy was that easy, I know that it isn't. The truth is that when we adopted our daughter, we were only doing what we had been led to do. If anyone qualifies for sainthood in our home, it would most likely be the child who has passed through the fiery furnace of human suffering.

If doing the right thing is what motivates you to adopt a child, you are not alone. But it is difficult indeed to keep doing the right thing through every turn in the road and every moment of our lives with an adopted child. Those who take the risk to act in charity are likely to discover just how selfish and unloving we can be—and are. To keep charity, we must guard it from what may destroy it. We can only do that if we set our hearts on the child we are choosing to love.

God is the source of all goodness. The Eternal One is the origin of every good thing we possess: our food and shelter, our clothing—even our morning coffee—come from God. Moreover, God is the fountain of every good deed we do. Every act of kindness and beauty (especially those that aren't random or senseless!), originates in the Ultimate Goodness that is God. The Lord provides for us, knowing what we need even before we ask. He does so every day, for our Creator is also our Sustainer.

Our Lord, however, is not just a divine benefactor, but also our heavenly Father. As Father, God is the source of everyone we love, everyone we have ever needed or relied on, everyone—period. Not content to help us in this life alone, the Lord calls us to be part of an eternal family. Not satisfied with merely assisting us from a distance, God promises us an everlasting home in his presence. Every one of us was made with that glorious destiny in mind. Our divine Father knew that without him we would all be orphans. Apart from our "Abba," none of us has what we need.

Holy Spirit, Fire of Charity, set our hearts ablaze. Work your love in our lives, your will in our plans, your holiness in our souls. Teach us to desire what is good and

right, and by your love, help us to bring your love to all. Keep us humble on the way. Protect us from pride and pity, from feeling that we are better, or more deserving, than anyone else. Inspire us to answer your call, and only your call, with prudence and patience. O Divine Flame, purify our motives and uproot everything in us that may be self-centered or self-serving. Perfect your love in us and through us. Lead us to those whom we are intended to love especially. Bless us and all our children with the warmth of your presence. Amen.

2

Called to Be Family
Choosing to Love

So (Naomi) said, "See, your sister-in-law has
gone back to her people and to her gods;
return after your sister-in-law." But Ruth said,
"Do not press me to leave you or to turn back
from following you! Where you go, I will go;
where you lodge, I will lodge; your people
shall be my people, and your God, my God."
— Ruth 1:15–16

$\mathscr{T}$he idea of adopting a child came to my husband and me gradually. Like land first appearing on
the horizon, the silhouette of what we saw grew larger
with every passing day. Detail, however, was impossible
to see from such a distance. We did not know all that
adoption would take, nor did we fully appreciate all that
it would demand of us. With seven notches in our parenting belts, our kids' doctor joked that we'd had more

experience with children than most pediatricians. Yet, we sensed that raising an adopted child could present us with an entirely different set of challenges than we had faced with our biological children. (We had no idea how right we were!) In the haze out at sea, idealism was a ready companion. The realities of the process and the changes that adopting a child would bring to our lives were sketchy at best.

One thing, however, was very clear: adoption came to us as a distinct call. Both my husband and I felt an inexplicable pull. Suddenly, we were inundated with adoption related "infomercials." In numerous personal encounters, Andrew and I heard all kinds of adoption stories. When complete strangers started offering personal anecdotes, I wondered if someone had stuck a sign on my back saying "Talk to Me About Adoption." Even the Scripture readings at church were strangely relevant. All that summer long we heard passage after passage about how God cared for orphans and heard their cries, how children would be gathered into one house from every corner of the earth, and how we were all the adopted children of a divine and heavenly Father. Everything seemed to relate to adoption. At times, it felt as if we had been whisked away to some kind of adoption theme park!

As the seriousness of our considerations increased, the call to adopt became louder, clearer, and less escapable. While we knew all along that the choice was ours to make, there seemed to be little question about what that choice would ultimately be. It was as if a path was being cleared before us. God, the divine Bushwacker, was very much on the move. We just had to figure out how to follow—and keep up.

Adoption is the deliberate choice to extend the natural boundaries of family life. Stretching to make any family inclusive takes work. In our home, it did not happen all at once, but continues one step at a time. Those steps are daily choices that sometimes don't feel much like choices at all. For our family, being convinced of our call to adopt has been an important refuge in times of frustration and struggle. In those moments when the stretch toward love has seemed beyond our reach, we have found reassurance in simply remembering that we adopted our daughter not only because we wanted to, or decided to, but because we were called—even *asked*—to do so.

At the root, love is always and essentially *optional.* A couple decides to accept one another as they are, to love no matter what, and to commit to growth that brings them closer together. All of that leads to choices that are even more fundamental. We choose to forgive, to respond rather than react, and to pace ourselves for love over a lifetime.

In these ways, the dynamic of adoption is a lot like that of marriage. When we choose to marry, we decide to love for life. We take on one another's strengths and weaknesses, not so much to change them, but to share in bearing them. A couple doesn't start off as one, but over the years becomes one by becoming one another's. Marriage is a call, a vocation to self-giving love. The same things can be said of adoption.

Not infrequently, the spark of adoption originates with one spouse and then spreads to the other. Sometimes the key is simply making a choice to slow things down in order to allow *both* prospective parents enough time and space for discernment. A decision as life changing as adopting a child must be made in unity and in peace. Truly, there is no need to rush. You may be convinced beyond a doubt that God is calling you to adopt a child. The love required to build a strong family, however, can be undermined if one spouse manipulates—or capitulates to—the other. Adoption should be the result of adult consensus, not compromise. Underneath it all, we know that the family we desire is not likely to be built on the ruins of the one we already have.

In the Scripture story, Ruth had a choice to make too. Her husband was dead, her sister-in-law had decided to go back to her original people and ways, and Naomi, her mother-in-law, was on the move as well. Free from any formal obligation, Ruth could choose any path without fear of judgment. There was no "wrong" choice. She was no longer bound to a husband or his family; nor was she tied to the world she had left

when she married from among another people. If she
went back to Moab no one would blame her. Knowing
what to expect—and what would be expected of her—
Ruth could take her place among familiar surround-
ings, perhaps a little wiser for what she had experienced among foreigners.

But that is not what Ruth would do. Instead of
reaching back to erase what had happened to her, she
chose to push ahead. Love would not let her return.
The same love that had called her to marry outside her
own people, now called her forward to accompany the
mother-in-law who had embraced her. Love is always a
choice, and always one that involves both a leaving
behind and a going forth. Ruth chose not only to go
with Naomi, but to leave her own home, her own people, even her own gods behind. She could not have
been sure of what the future would hold. Nonetheless,
Ruth chose to make all that was Naomi's her own.

For reasons beyond our understanding, God chooses to be a Father to us. There is nothing that forces the
Lord to do so. We are not the Master's only creatures,
but God has not made himself a Father to stars or
trees, butterflies or horses. We know this because the
Son of God, Jesus Christ, became one of *us.* In Christ,
God chooses to go forth with us. The Eternal Word,
leaving the glory of heaven behind, "became flesh" (Jn
1:14). Christ Jesus is able to sympathize with our weak-

nesses, for he has "been tested as we are, yet without sin" (Heb 4:15b).

Every family is called to be what the household of heaven is: a haven of love and life. Families who adopt have experienced adoption as a calling, but it is by no means a universal, impersonal, or indiscriminate call. Love is intensely personal. The deepest call we have in our lives is to share our lives with others. In learning to do so, our families become much more than the sum of their parts. Living in love and through love, we can become a *communion* of persons that reflects the very nature of our Triune God.

Holy Spirit, Spirit of Unity, help us to hear the call that draws us together. Empower us to speak "family" to one another, that the voice of the Father may echo not only in our hearts, but in our lives. Guide our considerations and our choices. Inspire us to look forward and beyond the boundaries of ourselves. Help us not only to know what you are asking of us, but to follow it to completion. Keep our feet on the way of love, and our hearts at the center of your will. Be with us, Holy Spirit, and, even more, be with all our children, those we know and love, and those whom we have yet to meet. Amen.

3

Longing for Life
Infertility

> When Rachel saw that she bore Jacob no
> children, she envied her sister; and she said
> to Jacob, "Give me children, or I shall die!"
> Jacob became very angry with Rachel and
> said, "Am I in the place of God, who has with-
> held from you the fruit of the womb?"
>
> — Genesis 30:1–3

*F*or some reason, families with more than three
children are considered amusingly odd. I can't remember the number of times someone has chortled, "Better
you than me!" (After a good look at them I usually
agree.) The ribbing my husband endures on a regular
basis has been more than enough to make him blush.
Of course, there is also an undercurrent of hostility we
don't have to dig very deeply to find. Suffice it to say
that we make an effort to avoid cars with bumper stick-

ers that mention overpopulation. I've sometimes thought about putting one on our car that reads: "If more people had more children, there'd be enough social security to go around!"

Having a large family has also made us particularly attuned to the pain of infertile couples. When we are out and around together, I have seen momentary flashes of anguish on some faces. At times it has been intense enough to make me aware that for some, our family is a glaring reminder of what they do not have. Eight children is an embarrassment of riches.

The demands we deal with on a daily basis can be more than a little overwhelming. Still, I know that on days when I've had enough of family life, there are many people who would happily feast on just a tablespoon of what I have. As amazing as it might seem to me, on any given day there are people who would be overjoyed to take my place if only they could—at least for a day or two, or until the laundry hampers overflowed! In my better moments that realization fills me with gratitude.

Somewhere in the midst of the suffering an infertile couple bears, the notion of adopting a child may come to mind. Often, the initial idea is dismissed too hastily. Some infertile couples feel that adopting a child is an admission of reproductive failure, but in truth, adoption is not a choice to give up on pregnancy. Many infertile couples who adopt eventually end up giving birth as well. Others, however, may see adoption as the acceptance of what they consider second-best or even as a last resort. Adoptive children, of course, are not inferior to "natural" ones. Both biological and adoptive parents think their children are the very best. And they're right!

On the other end of the spectrum are people who view adoption as a ready "fix" to a couple's "problem." The choice to adopt, however, is quite different. It is a choice to welcome a child who under any other circumstance would not be part of your life. Adoption is a meeting of hearts that long to love and to be loved. The pain of not being able to have children is very deep and very real. The pain of not having parents is also very deep and real.

It is no wonder that Jacob's most-beloved Rachel suffered such intense pain and inner desperation over childlessness. Neither is it surprising that she became envious of her very fertile sister, Leah. Running to Jacob, Rachel begs him to give her children. She fears that she will indeed die, unable to perpetuate her life by giving life to a child. Jacob responds to her from the well of his own pain and becomes angry. Startled by Rachel's near accusation that he has somehow withheld children from her, Jacob does not accept the blame for her infertility. God, he says, is responsible, and he hints that there may be some reason.

Apart from Jacob's anger, his response to Rachel is not without merit. All being and all life—both natural and supernatural—come from God. God is the origin and destiny of every living thing—the great Giver of gifts. Each of us is God's beneficiary. We have all received from heaven's abundance. The temptation, though, is to look at the Giver through the lens of what we want; that is, of what we do not yet have.

Over time, focusing on what we don't have makes us unhappy with our lives as a whole. It also contributes to the mistaken notion that we are somehow entitled to whatever we want. Fertile or infertile, no one has a "right" to a child. The truth is that while we may intensely desire children, while we may hope and plan for them, none of us is entitled to children. No one, including my husband and me, has done anything to "deserve" them.

Children, on the other hand, do have legitimate claims on their parents. Every child has the right to be conceived in love, raised in a stable family, have access to medical care, adequate food and shelter, and to be given an education and a foundation in moral and spiritual truths. Sadly, we know that not all children will have what they need or deserve.

Human persons, created in the image of God and to bear the divine image, long to create as God does: to pass life on to others and to perpetuate who and what we are. Faith teaches us that one of the supreme gifts of marriage is children, as they actually incarnate married love. That is not said lightly or as if there were no other marital gifts. Marriage is so rich that to communicate the depth of that richness we must incarnate it. That is, husbands and wives give life to children as the living and eternal sign of marital love and self-gift.

While adoption may not be a "solution" to anyone's "problem," it may well be an answer to a couple's prayers or the prayers of a homeless child. The challenge is to let go of what we do not have. If we can shift our focus from what it seems God is withholding from us, we can begin to glimpse—and then receive—what he is offering. It is entirely possible that God, the giver of all life, is indeed giving children to those who are unable to give birth. Adoption may be one way that he does so.

Holy Spirit, Divine Comforter, heal our wounds, comfort our grief, sustain us in hope. Keep our spirits from being clouded by disappointment. Help us to find life where we are, to treasure life wherever we find it, and to bring your everlasting life to all we meet. Teach us to be grateful for what you have given us already, and open our hearts to receive all that you wish to give us still. O Giver of Life, lead us according to your will. Enable us to recognize your answers to our prayers. Make of our lives a nurturing womb, ready to receive, protect, and love. Watch over us and all the children you have given us: those here, in heaven, and any who await our embrace. Amen.

4

The Opinion Poll
Dealing with What Others Think

> For you are our father, though Abraham does
> not know us and Israel does not acknowl-
> edge us; you, O LORD, are our father, our
> redeemer from of old is your name.
>
> — Isaiah 63:16

As our own thoughts about adoption developed, it occurred to Andrew and me that private reflection could give us the advantage of thinking things
through without the pressure or distractions that
come from open discussion. Unlike a pregnancy, it is
completely possible to keep a budding adoption entirely under wraps. Rather than thinking out loud, we
decided to involve relatively few people in our discernment process. Part of me just wanted to press ahead
without consulting anyone. My more deliberative hus-

band, however, did his best to rein in my highly motivated go-get-'em self.

Ultimately, we both knew that in order for any adoption to succeed, we would have to get all the important people, all the genuine participants, on board. Part of the challenge was to correctly discern just who was important and what weight to give to any individual's response. It took discipline not to share our snowballing excitement, but the effort was well worth it. Keeping the matter to ourselves enabled us to really hear what the people who mattered most had to say. A season of silence kept our own thinking focused, and made it possible to be responsive to the people that an adoption would impact most: the family we lived with every day.

We were convinced that if adopting a child was something that God was leading us to do, we would hear the divine voice in the responses of the people closest to us. I remember gingerly raising the topic with my mother and grandmother, not really knowing where either of them would stand. Because they live with us, their lives would also be affected by any child we would adopt. As much as I would have liked to think otherwise, I knew that it would be unfair to simply inform the other adult members of our household that we had decided to adopt. Instead, I confided in them. With all my fingers and toes crossed, I asked them what they thought and how they felt about the idea.

Prepared to hear legitimate opposition, I was delighted to find that both my mother and grandmother were very supportive.

At that time, we were hashing out all kinds of adoption options. Without carving any particular plan into stone, Andrew and I widened the circle of discernment to our children. Recognizing that any child we brought home would be one of them, we decided to grant each of our children the equivalent of veto power. Despite our desires, we were careful to reassure them that we would not move ahead with an adoption if any of them were really opposed to it. Each of our children would have to be willing to accept an adopted child into their fold.

Over the course of the summer, we talked with each of our kids individually, asking them to join us in the decision process. Some of our kids (those more like my husband) asked important questions and took time to think things through. Others (more like myself) couldn't jump on the adoption bandwagon fast enough. We encouraged them to share any concerns they had, and listened to every point they raised. If honest opposition or discomfort was voiced within our own family, we were prepared to interpret it as a heavenly red light to what we were considering. What we got was one green light after another.

We didn't go public with our intention to adopt until we knew that our whole family was of one mind in support of it. When we did, we were surprised by the reactions we received. Sufficient support was not hard to find, but it was not always where we thought we would find it. Andrew's co-workers, for example, were much more positive and interested than we had ever imagined. Later, when we returned home with our daughter, some even brought her "welcome home" gifts. A year later, one of them ended up adopting a little boy from Russia! The overwhelming majority of our friends and associates were supportive at varying levels. Some people told us about their own family adoption stories; others just listened to our plans with a smile. Still others offered concrete and much-appreciated help.

There was another group of people, however, quick to pass on every adoption horror story they had ever heard. One woman told me about a family that had adopted a girl from Korea who turned out to be mentally ill. Another recounted a story of an adopted boy who was abusive toward other children in the family. Quite a few people observed that adopted children never really fit into their families, that they *all* have emotional issues, and that most of them are disabled in some way. One woman even went so far as to warn me that all of "those children from Russia" were "special needs." With great conviction they shared many of their own fears and prejudices. Alarmed at first, we came to realize that most of what these peo-

ple offered us flowed from a mixture of genuine concern and simple ignorance. Eventually, we were able
to identify the people with whom we could comfort-
ably share our journey, as well as those with whom we
could not. Most were happy to come along, or at least
watch, in joy.

Like it or not, the choice to adopt a child meets
with a varied and plentiful response. It may be liberat-
ing to know that a person's reaction to your plan to
adopt a child does not have to be a litmus test for your
relationships. In dealing with other people's opinions,
we discovered that perhaps more than any other quality, adoption demands imagination. Adoption requires
us to recognize and act on something we cannot see;
namely, that there is a child somewhere who is meant
to be ours. Not everyone around us is able to visualize
things in that way.

No adoption plan meets with universal acclaim or
universal opposition, but opinions do change. Over time,
several people who started off negative developed a more
positive disposition toward what we were doing. Some
even became enthusiastic. As the abstract theory of adoption became the concrete reality of welcoming a particular child, ideas and opinions evolved. Ours did, too.
Everything we planned about our adoption melted away
in the light of our daughter's face. Suddenly, those agen-
das no longer mattered. What did matter was the child in
front of us, the one *God* had planned for us all along.

God mysteriously lays claim to every one of us. Every human being is, in reality, part of the whole human family. This holds true even in the face of those who would find some reason to deny it. Each one of us can claim God as our Father. God's other children may not know or acknowledge us in any way. We ourselves may even fail to recognize who we truly are. God, however, remains our Father nonetheless.

Things are not always what they seem to be, mostly because there is much we cannot see. Beneath the surface of our lives, however, is a flowing river of truth from which we can draw if we dare. Faith is our water jar. Entrusting ourselves to the God who sees everything helps us not only to see reality, but to imagine beyond what we see. Faith teaches us to gaze rather than glance. It gives us vision that is more than human, vision that is a glimpse of how God sees things, not twenty/twenty, but eternity/eternity.

Every family who chooses to adopt understandably longs to share their expectant joy with family and friends. Not everyone, however, will embrace the path. There are people in your life who can run alongside you with abandon. Some can join you for only part of the way. Others, for reasons of their own, will not be able to join you at all. But around the next turn, there are people you will meet, people who are sent by the Holy Spirit to give you exactly what you need when you need it, and only because you seek to adopt a child.

Holy Spirit, Spirit of Understanding, speak your will clearly in our hearts. Help us to recognize your voice in what we hear, and grant us the grace to listen attentively. Give us the ability to imagine, to trust what we cannot yet see, and to walk by faith. O Heavenly Comforter, send us all the encouragement we need. Guard the joy you have given us from the words of those who cannot share it. Uphold us as your children, and teach us to affirm your will in others' lives, even when we don't understand it. Be with us until our journey ends, and befriend the children who wait for us. Amen.

5

Making Connections
Selecting an Agency

"And I will ask the Father, and he will give you
another Advocate."

— John 14:16

*T*he next item on our to-do list was selecting an
adoption agency. It seemed a straightforward enough
task, until my internet search produced a list of over
three million matches. Clicking through the first few
pages, I couldn't imagine being able to choose an
agency with any more assurance than if I had picked a
name out of a hat.

My husband and I decided that I would take on the
exploratory stage solo. One person diving into the
ocean of listings and endless details was enough.
Someone had to breathe for both of us. Day after day, I
plunged into the names and lists and sites. I read as

much information as I could about how to select an agency. I researched different options—including adopting without an agency—until I ran out of air. Surfacing, it seemed to me that the process was more arbitrary and random than I had hoped. That realization was disconcerting to both of us.

While it seemed that there were genuine differences between agencies, we were at a loss as to how to determine whether those variables were significant or not. Actually, we really didn't know what an adoption agency was supposed to do. That made evaluating the relative advantages they highlighted a nearly impossible task. Some agencies were large, others small. Some were strictly domestic, others specialized in one or more foreign countries. There were those that had a definite religious feel, and others that maintained a purely secular image. Costs varied, but not as widely as did the amount of time an adoption would take.

The initial application forms were very different. Some agencies required not much more than name and address. Others asked detailed questions about child-raising and even the hopes and aspirations parents had for the child they sought to adopt. There were agencies that seemed to advocate more strongly for one side of the process: some for the needs of the child, and others for the desires of the prospective parents. Still others attempted a more balanced approach to family "match-making." All had references available upon request.

The task of choosing an agency felt like playing "Pin-the-tail-on-the-donkey." Blindfolded and dizzy, we asked God to put us into the right hands. There was no real way of making a decision with that many options and possibilities. In the end, I whittled the choices down to a short list of three, although the criteria I used to eliminate the others were much more intuitive than rational. Moving forward, I contacted those three agencies with information about who we were and what we hoped to do. In the process, I began to see what some of these agencies' differences meant in how an adoption played out.

The next step was checking references. Most, of course, were glowing, but the one review that wasn't caught my attention. Usually, someone else's negative experience would be reason enough for me to make my list even shorter. But this time, it just didn't feel fair. I knew no adoption agency could please 100 percent of its clients 100 percent of the time. Instead of eliminating the agency on the basis of one unfavorable review, I decided to give them the chance to tell their side of the story. I reported to the agency the complaint I had read, and Doris, the agency director, spoke forthrightly and honestly about what had gone wrong. More importantly, she did not express any lingering negativity toward the dissatisfied family. Her response sold us.

After giving due diligence to the substantive differences between agencies, we made a choice by listening to our hearts: a small family-run agency in Oklahoma that specialized in adoptions from Russia.

Although we knew being comfortable with our adoption agency would be a valuable asset, we did not fully appreciate just how much so until we were abroad. Traveling, we met several families who were far less than confident in the agencies they worked with. But on the far side of the globe, we found more reason to question ourselves than to doubt our agents. We knew that our representatives were just that—ours. They fully understood our motivation to adopt and the perspective from which we pursued adoption. Our agency acted not only for us, but with us.

Because adopting a child is a personal and lifelong journey, trusting others' advice and expertise is not always easy. We all come to the adoption process with a purpose—and perhaps a calendar—in mind. That purpose often involves much more than simply bringing home a child. All of us have hopes and dreams for our children, even for those who are not yet ours. We also have expectations of the process itself.

Selecting an adoption agency is one choice that will affect almost every other aspect of your adoption. In essence, you are choosing a Sherpa to accompany you on the climb, a guide for your journey into unknown territory where the air—and the ice—can be thin in places. And while it may not seem so at the time, you are selecting a particular process as well. In the end, most people choose an agency that feels right. Practical considerations are important, but not nearly as critical as being convinced that you are working with people whom you believe are worthy of your trust.

While most of what adoptive parents seek is reasonable, some things we hope for may not be completely realistic. Every family has areas in which its members can be flexible, and those in which they dare not be. For example, we knew that adopting a child with serious medical conditions would not be prudent for our family. But what we didn't know, until we met our daughter, was that we didn't really *need* to adopt an infant. Age was something we could be flexible about. A good agency will assist prospective parents in the wise discernment of matters that arise over the course of an adoption. Further, it will do so in a way that is attentive to that family's particular needs and desires. An open relationship with an adoption agency can form the foundation not only for advocacy, but assistance, consolation, and encouragement along the way. For us, the positive relationships we built along the way added to the joy on our journey.

God rarely asks us to do things alone. Almost without exception, our callings are beyond us, or rather beyond *just* us. The Holy Spirit's promptings usually require us to go out of ourselves. While we easily acknowledge that living by faith means reaching out to others, we tend not to envision ourselves as needing

assistance. Often, however, the most deeply spiritual times of our lives, the experiences that truly transform us, are those in which we are uncomfortably dependent on the help others are willing to give. When we struggle with illness, job loss, or the death of someone close to us, we find ourselves on the receiving end of charity. When Andrew was out of work for three years, for example, we discovered how very important it was to have both faith and friends.

God never leaves us in the lurch—at least not for long. God helps us readily, not from a distance, but from within our own hearts. This wonderful Spirit of God, alive in our souls, assists us even when we do not know how to ask for help; perhaps even when we do not know we need help. It is no coincidence that the Holy Spirit is called the Paraclete: the helper, comforter, intercessor, the one who is called to aid us. Jesus promised his disciples that they would have "another Advocate," because he knew that they would need one.

The God who created families in the first place continues to build them. Our heavenly Father is no less involved in adoption than he is in birth, and at times, more visibly so. All families are a divine work of grace. Whatever connections you use to adopt, the Holy Spirit is your invisible adoption agent and facilitator, the unseen coordinator of the process you will undertake, and the power behind your ability to complete it. This divine and life-giving Spirit of the Most High does not operate by means of waiting lists and application forms, but by love and in the fullness of time.

Holy Spirit, Friend of Souls, we place ourselves in your hands. Lead us to those who will help us. Empower us to trust in your care and in those who will make the journey with us. Work your will in every part of the process we are about to undertake. Teach us patience and perseverance. Give us confidence in your word to us, and in all the unseen aspects of our lives. O Paraclete, inspire us to advocate for others, to support and encourage them to follow the paths they take. Be our unfailing connection to heaven and to all our children. Even before we know who or where they are, bind us together in your love. Amen.

6
A Passing Grade
Homestudy

> Do your best to present yourself to God as
> one approved by him, a worker who has no
> need to be ashamed, rightly explaining the
> word of truth.
>
> — 2 Timothy 2:15

Seeking approval for adoption didn't bother me,
but the idea of having a social worker come to our
house did. For some reason, being evaluated scared me.
I felt a tension that I hadn't perceived before—a tension
between wanting to *be* good and feeling like I needed
to *look* good. Anticipating some of the questions
we might be asked, Andrew and I knew all we had to
do was tell the truth. Somehow, that didn't seem as
simple as it should. We found it hard to be fair to ourselves. Andrew tended to understate our strengths and

overemphasize our weaknesses. I pulled in precisely the opposite direction. It wasn't that we didn't know ourselves, just that neither of us was completely satisfied with falling short of our own standards.

When I first spoke on the phone with Laura, our homestudy worker, I was extremely nervous. The truth is that after almost eighteen years of adult responsibility, I was dreadfully afraid of not making the cut. I held my cards close to my chest, put on my best telephone voice (the one I never use with my kids), and made sure that there would be absolutely no interruptions. Laura already knew that we had seven biological children. Strangely, that fact didn't seem to deter her. Happily sketching out the process of visits, paperwork, and the overall homestudy calendar, Laura seemed enthusiastic about our plan to adopt and our purpose in doing so. When she told me that she had adopted her own son from Guatemala, I began to feel more at ease. Laura seemed nice enough, but I really wasn't sure about how far to let my guard down. At the end of our conversation, I asked her if she saw herself as more of a gatekeeper or an advocate. When she answered "advocate," I stopped holding my breath, scheduled a home visit, and started cleaning.

When Laura arrived, she was every bit as positive in person as she had been on the phone. She didn't seem concerned about how clean everything was, nor did she seem to be looking for reasons to keep us from adopting what all her paperwork referred to as "an infant child from Russia." Gathering everyone together after her tour of the house and initial interview, Laura asked our kids about our plan to adopt. After fielding their rather excited responses, she simply said, "Let's do it!" Our interviews after that felt a lot more like conversation between friends.

Self-gift is the heart of adoption. Whenever we present ourselves, we make a present of ourselves. That is why a homestudy can be a bit unsettling—we're afraid that our "present" may be rejected as inadequate. Obviously, someone has to protect the interests of children by making sure they are adopted by families who can, and will, provide for them. Reasonable people recognize that it is necessary to assess prospective parents and their environments. Nevertheless, it is natural to feel anxious when you are the one being evaluated—I certainly did! Families who already have children worry about whether the results of their parenting will make the grade. Couples seeking to become parents through adoption are concerned about their ability to convince someone they hardly know that they would be ideal mothers and fathers.

There is no need to fear, however. No family is perfect, especially those who look like they might be! Every family has its share of both shining virtues and glaring deficiencies. In spite of this, I have never heard of a family being denied a recommendation to adopt.

The process of homestudy is one of family self-discovery. Those who view it as just a necessary inconvenience—a bureaucratic hoop to jump through—will miss a valuable opportunity for personal assessment. The information you will be required to provide can help you to identify and acknowledge both your strengths and weaknesses. Homestudy encompasses just about every aspect of life that could impact an adopted child: finances, job security, marital stability, medical issues, personal support systems, cultural awareness, prospective parents' own personal development, commitment to education, and attitudes toward adoption and parenting. Having all that data at hand can give you a clear picture of where you are. It can also provide the motivation to follow through on some of those things you've always meant to address, like cleaning the garage or making a will. More than anything else, however, the process of homestudy establishes a professional support relationship that serves as an adoptive family's first link to resources they probably never even knew existed. Laura, for example, was able to give us solid guidance regarding our daughter's development and bonding. And later, in post-placement visits, she provided a good reality check for our expectations.

While the overwhelming majority of homestudy providers work very hard to facilitate adoption, there are rare instances in which the underlying philosophy or values of the social worker clash dramatically with those of the family. If an unproductive dynamic does arise, it is best to address it directly and without delay. Prospective parents who feel judged rather than evaluated, or experience a genuine disconnect in open communication, should not be afraid to engage another professional.

In our culture of (rarely constructive) criticism and judgment, it may be helpful to remember that Shakespeare was wrong: the world is not really a stage on which life is "played"; nor are our relationships one long audition for a production in which some are given starring roles and others are stuck backstage struggling to keep the spotlight on others. We need not be too concerned with how our reviewers receive us, or even how we perceive our own performance. Ultimately, God is our audience. The Lord's approval is the only one any of us really needs. And, as St. Paul puts it, "If God is for us, who can be against us?" (Rom 8:31b)

In seeking our heavenly Father, we can reveal who we are with great confidence. The Scriptures tell us to seek God as people already approved by him. Those who seek divine approval are empowered to do so because they already have it. Living our lives from a sense of being accepted by God changes everything. Suddenly, we have nothing to prove and no enemies to fear. We are free to forgive ourselves, free to laugh at ourselves, and free to give ourselves fully to the Lord.

Faith is the answer to doubt, even to self-doubt. If we listen to our hearts, we may hear the inner dialogue between the voices of what we are and what we used to be, wish we were, or hope to become. In the midst of that inner conversation, the Holy Spirit speaks a word of encouragement and freedom. That still, small voice assures us that we need not be concerned about how we compare to other people or how we stack up against our own standard of perfection. God wants us to be inspired by his ideals, not worried sick over them. Our heavenly Father is far more concerned with where we are headed than with where we are, and even less concerned with where we have been in the past. More than with us, God is for us.

Holy Spirit, Mighty Advocate, thank you for loving us the way we are. Help us to see ourselves as you see us, and to share who we truly are with others. Enable us to know the truth about our gifts and limitations, and to commend that truth to your care. Forgive us our sins, and teach us to forgive ourselves and others. O Sanctifying Love, sustain us on the way of holiness and perfection. As we become what you made us to be, give us confidence in your approval. Reassure us with your presence, and help us to affirm the children you have given—and will give—into our care. Amen.

7

Matters of Privacy
Open vs. Closed Adoption

"These are the words of the holy one, the true
one, who has the key of David, who opens and
no one will shut, who shuts and no one opens:
I know your works. Look, I have set before you
an open door, which no one is able to shut."
— Revelation 3:7b–8a

When we decided to adopt, we knew that whatever approach we took would affect not only the child we brought home, but also the children already at home. We experienced our calling as one to extend the family we had built by integrating into it an adopted child. As tempting as the idea was at times, we didn't really intend to start our own orphanage or change the world. For us, adoption was a way to share our family life, not an opportunity to remodel it. We envisioned all our children—biological and adoptive—sharing the same

43

set of relationships. We didn't want a radical change in family life for the seven kids we already had.

Our family's structure and dynamics, as in any large family, were already firmly established, almost to the point of being a subculture. Because we are raising so many children, the time necessary to maintain relationships is always at a premium, so incorporating members of an adopted child's birth family into our own family life was not a viable choice for our household. The thought of explaining such a complex network of relationships to children of a wide assortment of ages and understanding was overwhelming. Trying to imagine the confusion that would result made my head spin. Not even a switchboard operator would be able to keep track of who was who to whom!

Adoption is a profoundly personal matter that involves the private lives of a number of people. As one might expect, there are numerous viewpoints about how to handle sensitive information in a respectful manner. The debate between those who advocate agreements at the opposite poles of the adoption spectrum does not provide much assistance to prospective parents. What parents need to know is that there is no single best or right way to adopt a child. Almost any arrangement can work well, if boundaries regarding privacy are mutually accepted and respectfully maintained.

"Closed" adoption is understood to be an exclusive transfer of the child's family bonds to his or her adoptive family. The identities of both the birth and adoptive parents are protected from each other and—through public records—from the adopted child. In a closed adoption, birth parents surrender custody to an agency or other legal guardian, and relinquish decisions about who will raise their child. Neither they nor their extended families take an active role in the child's life. Because of this, relatively little information about the child's background is made available to the adoptive family.

"Open" adoption is understood to be an inclusive sharing of the child's family bonds between members of both birth and adoptive families. Generally speaking, an adoption is considered fully open if birth parents have a say in their child's placement, and the families involved arrange direct and ongoing contact between an adopted child and members of his or her birth family. In practice, there are varying degrees of "openness." In some instances, the birth mother's participation ends with choosing her child's adoptive parents. More often, though, an agreement is negotiated regarding the nature and frequency of her ongoing contact with the child she places. Such interaction can be direct or mediated through the adoption agency. It is not uncommon for an agency to pass letters and photographs or even to arrange visits at parks or other public facilities. Full identities and addresses of birth and adoptive parents may be shared—or not—between them.

Most of the debate over what form of adoption is best centers on opinions regarding whom it is best for. By and large, closed adoption creates a condition that many consider more favorable to adoptive parents. Once the adoption is final, parents are free to raise their son or daughter without input or influence of any kind. On the other hand, many view more open adoptions as preferable to a child's family of origin and to birth mothers in particular. For many, the structure of an open adoption is the difference between "giving up" a child and lovingly placing a child into someone else's care. Instead of abdicating maternal responsibility altogether, an open adoption allows the birth mother an active and ongoing role in her child's life at a level of responsibility that she is capable of sustaining.

Every form of adoption offers the child a particular set of advantages. Proponents of closed adoption place a high value on the stability that comes from clearly defined family relationships. Their concern is that children who grow up with two sets of parents may experience a sense of divided loyalty or confusion. Those who advocate open adoption believe that keeping a child personally connected to his own history is an advantage. Their hope is that by maintaining relationships where possible, families may be more equipped to address the questions of identity that are often intensified for the adopted child.

Issues arise, however, from all types of adoption arrangements. Parents who choose a closed adoption believing that this will functionally eliminate the need to deal with a child's birth parents will find that they are mistaken. Adoptive families cannot avoid their child's birth parents—even if they never meet in person. Every adopted child lives with the consequences, both positive and negative, of his or her family relationships, even if the relationships are not ongoing. While our daughter, for example, easily recalls her life in the orphanage, she does not remember ever having a family. As a result, her interactions with us are sometimes colored by an understandable fear of being abandoned or alone.

On the other hand, parents who opt to include birth relatives in their child's upbringing may discover that agreements made are not always kept. Some families have struggled with birth parents or grandparents who seek more than the agreed-upon amount of personal contact with a child. Others have had to explain to their adoptive child why a birth parent has chosen to drop out of their lives. Adoptive parents may also find themselves less than enthusiastic about the influence a birth parent may have on their child's moral and spiritual development.

It is difficult to evaluate what kind of adoption is best for children. Even when everyone involved focuses on the long-term interests of the child, determining just what is best is not always possible. The trouble is that you may not be able to implement what is clearly "the best" adoption plan. Most international courts do not provide for open adoption. Many explicitly prohibit any contact between birth and adoptive families, even if both sides wish to establish it. Each child and every adoption situation is unique. Adoption is not a "one size fits all" proposition. Still, even the most flexible of legal systems has its limits.

The more we learn, the more we realize how little knowledge we possess. Thankfully, in life we can and do experience more than what we are able to fully comprehend. That is, while most of us *have* it, not many of us "get it!" Our relationship with God has this same quality. While we can know information about God, and even encounter the Lord in a personal way, the Eternal Being is far too mysterious for any of us to grasp completely. Ostriches and penguins have wings, but neither can fly. Likewise, we are limited by what we are.

It is astonishing that the God who has no limits never limits our access to his heart. Our heavenly Father is continuously available, forever open to us—even when we are not open to him. The Spirit of the Most High is always near, especially to those who call for assistance. No one can close what God opens, and the Lord chooses to open himself to all. Further, no one can open what God closes. That is, no one can uncover what God does not reveal. God is the divine Revealer as well as the subject of divine revelation.

The shape your adoption will take depends on the expectations you have for family life, and what you—as prospective parents—wish to welcome into it. Whatever kind of adoption you pursue, both birth and adoptive parents should be certain that they understand exactly what they are choosing. The members of each family must discern for themselves not just what conditions they are willing to accept, but what they are happy to live with. That is, parents ought to reflect on much more than what feels comfortable at the time. Their considerations should be undertaken with an eye toward what they believe will be genuinely good in the long run.

In the final analysis, all of us make decisions within the limits of our understanding and within the parameters of what is possible. Acting in faith, we trust that the positive aspects of what we choose are a good match for the needs of the individual child we embrace. Sustained by the Holy Spirit, we are empowered to make the most of every advantage we are given. Whatever doors we choose to close in the adoption process, we know that the door to our hearts must be left wide open. No one can teach us that kind of openness better than the God who is always open to receive us as beloved children.

Holy Spirit, Guiding Light, show us clearly the land where you would have us go. Lead us along the pathways of your perfect will to the place that you have promised us. Whether near or far, at home or abroad, be always at our side. Give us the strength we need to finish the journey we begin. Protect us as we travel, and help us to be gracious guests. Keep us mindful of all those we leave behind. Give us the grace to find you wherever we are, and to follow you rather than our own way. Bring us to the children you intend for us. Guide them and us safely home to one another, and together to your eternal kingdom. Amen.

8

Where in the World?

Domestic vs. International Adoption

Now the Lord said to Abram, "Go from your country and your kindred and your father's house to the land that I will show you."
— Genesis 12:1

When we decided to adopt a child, it was immediately clear to us that we were called to adopt internationally. Our intention was to take a child from the poorest of the poor, to snatch someone out of the worst set of prospects a child could face. Part of our thinking, too, was that we not take a child from adoptive parents who, for reasons of their own, wanted to adopt only from within the United States. Our initial choices were to explore an adoption from India, China, or Guatemala. One by one, all those doors closed. The

53

Indian government was intent on having their children adopted by ethnic Indians if at all possible. Furthermore, the high value that Indian society places on children meant that most orphans were cared for quite well. China passed a new law that summer prohibiting adoption by families with more than five children. Guatemala's process at the time was done almost exclusively through private attorneys. It soon became clear that none of these countries was meant to be a match for our family

After a few broken noses we learned that when doors slam in our face, it is often God's way of telling us that they are simply the wrong doors. Investigating adoption from other countries, we began to see that Russia was the clear choice for us. Probably the worst place on earth to be an orphan at the time, Russia had hundreds of thousands of homeless children crowded into facilities that did not even have enough food to feed them. Of those who did grow up in the system, only twenty percent would go on to live relatively normal lives. The rest ended up either in prison, on drugs, as prostitutes—or dead. Those harsh realities drew us like moths to a flame.

In addition, Russia made perfect sense for us from a cultural point of view. Because of my ethnic background, our family already celebrated Slavic holiday traditions. Despite my husband's typical American ethnic mix, our kids look Slavic as well. A Russian child would feel very much at home with us, hardly foreign at all. At family prayers, we began to intercede for "the baby on the other side of the world." Where that baby belonged, we figured, was with us.

Everything pointed to Russia, but Russia is an expansive nation, the largest in the world, in fact. Choosing to adopt in Russia was like saying that we had "narrowed it down" to finding a child in a country twice as big as our own. The real question was, where in Russia?

When our paperwork was done, our agency told us that we should expect to travel to a region called Astrakhan, on the Caspian Sea. I immediately looked up all the information I could find on that region's history, economy, and culture. I also researched adoption there. The more I learned about Astrakhan, the more excited I became. With stories of Tatars and the golden horde, it seemed to me an exotic place rich with mystery. I could practically taste the caviar!

Within days of our departure, however, I received a call from our agency. For some unknown reason, when our papers arrived in Russia, a decision was made to send us to Voronezh instead of Astrakhan. Voronezh, as I found out, was a city on the Don River, 350 miles south of Moscow. I didn't really know why, but I felt as if the rug had been pulled out from under me. It was amazing how very attached I had become to the idea of going to Astrakhan—a place I had never seen—so much so, that I grieved at having to go somewhere else. Only later did I fully realize the importance of that last-minute and unanticipated change of plans. God did not send us to Astrakhan, because our daughter wasn't there.

The who and how of every adoption is largely determined by the when and where. The child you will eventually bring home is "chosen" by a maze of eliminations that may seem rather arbitrary at times. For some parents, the sense that their adoption process is random at all is frightening. The best way to get beyond the distrust that the process can engender is to realize that the Holy Spirit is present and active in it. The child you find depends completely on where, and even when, you search. The twists and turns you will go though to bring your child home depend almost entirely on where he or she is, and the timing of your application to adopt. Procedures, timelines, legal requirements—even the long-term character of your adoption—are dictated by whatever mechanisms and customs are in place. Every region or state in every nation on earth has a distinct way of viewing adoption, and its own understanding of what is best for children. Rules and regulations concerning who may adopt and who may be adopted reflect a country's basic attitudes toward family.

Because there are no orphanages in the United States, domestic adoptions often involve foster care or legal guardianship, at least for a brief time. Many adoptive parents have been a child's foster parents. The United States is also one of the few places in which decisions to place a child into an adoptive family are frequently made even before the child is born. Birth mothers exercise a high level of control over where their children are placed. Because of this, interaction with a child's birth mother at some level is a generally accepted part of the process. The continued presence of biological parents or grandparents in the adopted child's life is a matter that is negotiated between birth and adoptive parents. Regular interaction can be rare or not at all, or include a full set of visitation arrangements.

Most domestic adoptions are at least somewhat "open"; that is, an adopted child is assured of having access to all his or her birth and adoption records. The wait for referral and placement can be long, and, in most cases, a significant amount of time must pass before an adoption is finalized. However, parents who adopt domestically know a great deal about their son's or daughter's background. And, too, the process allows for parents to adopt newborn babies.

Variations in the adoption process around the world are endless. Some countries do not allow prospective parents to adopt a child under one year of age. Practically none allow for newborn adoptions. The law provides most children adequate time to be considered for adoption by families in their own countries. Some governments, however, are just as happy to see their children adopted by foreigners. It is nearly impossible to adopt a Chinese boy, but in Russia, the wait for a girl is longer. Other restrictions apply to adopting parents. There are nations that exclude parents with disabilities, single persons, those who are "too young" or "too old." A few countries will escort a child to her new parents in the United States. Others require adoptive parents to stay in the child's home country for several weeks, or even months.

The paperwork required for international adoption is more involved, and the cost of travel can be significant. Parents adopting internationally must secure legal immigration and citizenship for their children. Language barriers, too, play a significant role in the process from start to finish, and require more adjustment for children adopted beyond infancy. Little or no information about birth parents may be given, and a child's medical information may be difficult to decipher. On the other hand, no information about adoptive parents is given to birth mothers. The process in most foreign countries is "closed," and legal finalization is immediate. Most parents complete an adoption in less than a year. Ours took less than six months.

Every aspect of the adoption process can be considered a plus or a minus. For some, the thought of traveling halfway around the world to adopt is exciting.

For others, it is terrifying. Andrew and I had always wanted to see Russia. Before we even met, I had enrolled in a year of Russian language, and he had registered for a course in Russian history. Both of us dreamed of visiting St. Basil's and the Kremlin, but neither of us ever imagined that we would be adopting a Russian child. Looking at the options through the lens of your family's individual needs and adoption perspective is the only way to see things clearly. Your own history or culture may draw you to a particular place. You may have a friend or relative who has adopted a child you have grown to love. Or you may know of a particular child who needs a home. There is no one path to adoptive parenthood that is traveled by all, or even most.

When Abram first heard God's call, he may well have scratched his head in wonder. I can only imagine how Abram had to build up enough courage to talk to his wife, Sarai, about what he had heard. Told to leave everything behind, he was asked to pack up his whole life—family, friends, livelihood—and move. But where were they supposed to go?

That, in fact, was the most puzzling aspect of the whole business. The call to leave was very clear; their destination, however, was anything but. This God was not simply asking them to pull up stakes and start over somewhere else. The Almighty was telling them to trust him completely: to trade the life they had made for

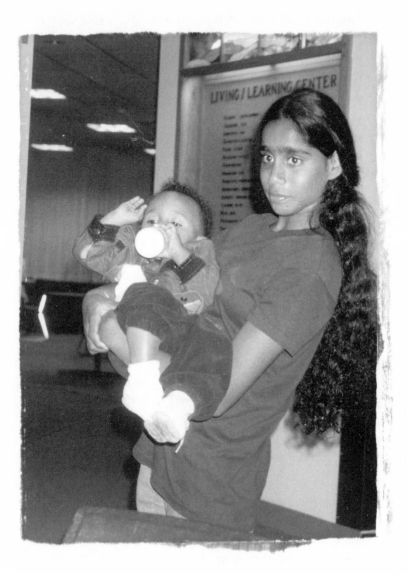

themselves for one that he would give them. From that moment on—even before they left—Abram and Sarai were no longer at home. Their place was no longer in the land of their birth, but in a land that God would show them, one the Lord had promised them.

As pilgrims in search of a home, Abram and Sarai became Abraham and Sara. Wanderers with no knowledge at all of where they were going or when and how they would get there, they must have wondered just how they were supposed to know when they had arrived. Certainly, there would be no one to greet them. They would find no sign carved into a cliff that said, "Welcome to Your New Home." We might be tempted to call this couple "directionless," but God called them "faithful."

Abraham and Sara were followers of the divine Will. Led by faith, they knew that the only truly secure place for them was under the shadow of God's wings. God does not tell us to move without showing us the way. However, unlike AAA members, we hardly ever get a "trip-tik" for the journey. God gives us only as much information as we actually need, never more, lest we stop trusting and following the lead of the Holy Spirit. Often, we are given only one step at a time—the next step we are meant to take. Thinking of God's call to us, many of us imagine traveling into the dark and distant unknown. The land that God will show us, however, is exactly that: the one that will be revealed to us as we go.

It is as likely to be far away as around the corner. Thankfully, our God is One who leads. The Holy Spirit will inspire and direct any who are willing to follow.

Holy Spirit, Wise Counselor, give us a clear understanding of the doors we have chosen to open and those that we have shut. Give us the grace to enter through the gate that you have chosen for us. Help us know what to expect and to be content in the process we pursue. Teach us to recognize hidden gifts, and sustain us in times of question or doubt. Empower us to be faithful to our commitments and to find in that faithfulness a source of joy. Guide us always forward in your will. Build our family in a way that will serve it well. Open our hearts to the children you will give us, and open their hearts to the love you have inspired for them in ours. Amen.

9

Celebrating Diversity
Cross-Racial and Cross-Cultural Adoption

Do not fear, for I am with you; I will bring your offspring from the east, and from the west I will gather you; I will say to the north, "Give them up," and to the South, "Do not withhold; bring my sons from afar, and my daughters from the ends of the earth, everyone who is called by my name, whom I created for my glory, whom I formed and made."

— Isaiah 43:5–7

When we began thinking about adoption, our first impulse drew us toward children from races and cultures very different from our own. We had resolved not to keep our child's adoption a secret from anyone; neither did we have any desire to "pass" an adopted child off as a biological one. I have to admit that the whole idea played well to the flakier aspects of my personality. Romanticizing the whole thing, I began to act as if international adoption was our own little diplomatic venture. Even though we intended to adopt only one child, I imagined how cute it would be for our family to become a miniature United Nations. I wondered how long it would take to teach the children to sing "It's a Small World."

As our considerations came down to earth, however, we realized that while race was not an issue for us, it very well could develop into an issue for the child we would adopt. With seven brothers and sisters sharing a high degree of family resemblance, racial difference could present our adopted child with a significant obstacle to identity and belonging. As our family dialogue continued, we also discovered that while all our children were more than willing to welcome a brother or sister of another race, some of them were not at all prepared to handle other people's racist responses.

One of our kids had once witnessed ill-mannered children tease their Korean school bus driver. The experience made him very apprehensive of interracial adoption. Recounting what he had seen, he told us that he just couldn't stand the thought of seeing a brother or sister being treated that way. Andrew and I were saddened that this sort of incident still happens in our country, but we listened to our son's concerns. Largely because of them, we chose to adopt a child from a racial and cultural background very close to our own.

More and more adoptive families have chosen to make cultural and racial differences less and less a factor in the decisions they make. Some have made race a primary concern, and have actively sought to build multiracial families. Others have accepted referrals for children of races other than their own even when they had not expected to do so.

Families who choose to adopt cross-racially or cross-culturally have a special set of considerations. It is important for all of us to recognize that racism does (still!) exist, and that the cross-racial adoptive family may well encounter it. Parents who have never had to worry about prejudice may be surprised to find just how pervasive it is in certain circles. Some may even experience it in members of their own extended families.

The tragedy of race discrimination affects individual children differently. For some, a racial difference between them and their parents or siblings is not an issue. For others, race looms large on the child's interpersonal horizon. An adopted minority child may project perceived racism onto situations in which it does not actually play a role. I know of one little girl who incorrectly concluded that she was not given the part she hoped for in a dance recital only because she is Chinese. Sadly, this child has felt unnecessarily uncomfortable. While she is strongly attached to her family, her keen sense of being different has made it difficult for her to integrate more fully into the larger community.

There is one additional point that parents considering cross-racial adoption should bear in mind. An obvious distinction in race between a child and his or her other family members means that the adoption itself cannot be kept private. The cross-racially adopted child does not have the luxury of choosing if—or when—to tell other people that he became a member of his family through adoption. Most "obviously adoptive families" I've met have started wondering whether people in grocery store check-out lines talk about anything other than adoption! Having such a personal matter made common knowledge can be a lot for children and their parents to carry. But together, parents and their children can turn their situation into an opportunity to witness to ever-broadening love. I know a foster family who has welcomed numerous children from all kinds of racial and cultural backgrounds. The mother is Lithuanian, the father Syrian; their four children have brothers and sisters who are Cambodian, Vietnamese, and African American. You can taste the love in their home—especially on homemade pizza night!

The cross-cultural aspects of adoption are distinct from racial matters. Even children who are of the same race as their adoptive parents can come from a radically different cultural background. Welcoming any child into your family means welcoming an entire history and heritage as well. Part of the joy of adoption is widening our cultural awareness and horizons. There are no ethnic requirements for enjoying refried beans, borscht, or lo mein. Personally, I like them all!

There are many ways for parents to keep an adopted child connected to his or her culture of origin. Native foods, music, language, and crafts can all be given a place of honor in the home. We have Russian icons in our home, and have attempted to make traditional Russian Easter eggs. Andrew and I continue to use at least a bit of the conversational Russian we learned. We've even served tea from a samovar. As we discover more cultural traditions, we will continue to include them in our home. Highlighting a child's background affirms that child's identity and self-understanding. Further, it is a way of giving the adopted child a fuller sense of roots than he or she might otherwise have. Cultural pride and connectedness is especially helpful to children who were adopted beyond infancy. For them, familiar foods, stories, songs, and artistic expression can provide an irreplaceable source of comfort and belonging.

Culture sharing affords families a rich avenue of mutual acceptance. Such exploration and exchange can flow joyously in two directions. I will never forget the absolute ecstasy our daughter expressed when she tried on the little Russian national costume I had bought for her. She was even more delighted when I tried mine on, too! Families who do what they can to participate in their child's culture should also feel free to fully share their own heritage. They should do so regardless of the child's racial or ethnic background. Our daughter has become the best little Russian step-dancer ever. And we have seen more than a few Asian girls dancing the jig as well!

The Holy Spirit is a Spirit of unity and love. That love has no borders or boundaries of any kind. From every direction, from every place, from every culture and language and race, God calls us as one people—simply because we belong to the Lord. We do not become the children of God at the moment when we are finally gathered to him. We are already the sons and daughters of the Creator. We are already called by the holy name of God even though we may be at the very ends of the earth. God is already our heavenly Father.

Diversity is a fact of life and the beauty of creation. Truly celebrating the richness of our differences, however, is not as simple or as easy as it sounds. The challenge is that in affirming diversity, we risk losing sight of the even deeper reality of what unites us. In treating everything "equally," we tend to avoid making the comparisons that enable us to recognize what is truly excellent in a particular culture.

While most of us relish the great variety of flowers and landscapes and birds, many of us have felt intimidated at times by diversity that is purely human. I may be comfortable talking about how people come in all shapes, colors and sizes. But all that philosophy does little to make me feel comfortable when I walk into a room where I'm the one who is "different."

Everybody is concerned about fitting in. Unfortunately, the world in which we live is not always helpful in this regard. It tells us in a thousand whispered ways that in order to fit we must conform. The expectation is that we will make ourselves essentially interchangeable.

God, however, has another point of view. Our Creator has made every one of us for divine glory. Each of us is tailor-made, made to fit. There is no doubt that we belong. But like pieces in a puzzle, our differences are what help us to discover where we belong—not just with God, but with one another.

Holy Spirit, Lord of all Nations, give us eyes that see the beauty of every culture and race. Stretch our hearts beyond the boundaries of birth, nation, and race, and help us to fully welcome your image in all people. Help us to see the unity that lies deeper than all diversity. Inculturate your eter-

nal kingdom in our hearts; where all are recognized as sons and daughters of the Father. Root out any racism that may linger in our souls, and give us the strength to act justly when we encounter it ourselves. Through the life we share with our children, reaffirm that love has no color, race, or nationality. Show us how to belong to one another and to you. Amen.

10

Choosing the "Unwanted"
Special-Needs Adoption

For everything created by God is good, and nothing is to be rejected, provided it is received with thanksgiving....
— 1 Timothy 4:4

*T*he very first form we filled out, our agency's initial application, asked us to list any kinds of special needs that we would be willing to accept in a child. I was somewhat surprised at what was on the list of disabilities. Crossed eyes, a cleft palate or lip, a missing finger or toe; some of these things seemed rather small. But there were also things on that list I considered enormous—things like autism, deafness, Hepatitis C, cerebral palsy, and HIV.

Honestly, the special needs question frightened me. On one hand, I felt guilty for wanting a healthy child.

On the other hand, I knew that the demands of our large family made choosing a particularly needy child unwise. Andrew and I simply did not have the time and energy a child with special needs deserved or would need. Given our limitations, we knew that we could not commit ourselves to major ongoing medical challenges. We were, however, willing to accept problems that could be corrected with medical intervention, as well as mild to moderate learning disabilities. We were also open to adopting a child from a "difficult" background such as extreme poverty, abuse, or neglect.

The list of what can be considered "special needs" is very long indeed. Likewise, the range of conditions and diagnoses is enormous. Some of these constitute the full explanation for why a particular child is available for adoption. Birth parents may not have either the personal and financial resources or support necessary to address their child's needs. It is not uncommon for children with correctable "defects" to be abandoned to the streets, especially in countries where surrendering a child is illegal, as in China. In some places, female infants are considered undesirable. More serious physical issues present steep obstacles for children who need homes.

A prospective family's concerns extend well beyond matters that pertain to physical health. Emotional damage due to neglect or abuse may bring into question a child's ability to develop healthy family relationships.

Social and behavioral issues related to a child's institu-
tionalization are also significant. Children who are
affected by severe fetal alcohol syndrome, Down's, or
autism, or who have a family history of mental illness,
are among those most difficult to place. Of course,
there are always people who regard adoption itself as
enough to classify a child as having "special needs"!
Some seem to think that simply having been adopted
damages a child for the rest of his or her life. This, however, is not a perspective most orphaned children could
share. Having a family is almost always better than not
having one.

Every child is good and worthy of life and love.
Those words come easily when we envision children
who are healthy; kids who can run and play and learn to
read; children we can be proud of and who bring us joy.
But such words don't always flow like milk from a bot-
tle. The truth is that many of us don't know what to say
to parents who give birth to a child with illness or disabilities. Thankfully, most of us do have a sense of compassion for families who find themselves suddenly fac-
ing challenges they did not anticipate. Far fewer of us,
however, can even begin to understand parents who
would deliberately seek to adopt a child whose health
or future looks less than promising.

Families who seek to parent a child with special
needs do so because they trust that among the thorny
challenges they face are rare and fragrant gifts. The

children they are called to adopt may be among the poorest and neediest, often those who have no one willing to help them. Whether through life experience or expertise, parents of children with special needs know the value of small accomplishments and the depth of simple joys. For them, a child taking his first steps at six years of age is as exciting—maybe more exciting—than a baby walking across the kitchen on her first birthday.

Parents of children with special needs, by either birth or adoption, stand against the prevailing sentiment of our culture. They are expert at separating the human condition from the human person. They do not view their children as burdens or disappointments. Many are deeply grateful even for those things that seem the most difficult aspects of their lives. One mother of a child with special needs told me her daughter had made her a better person. Accepting a child another couple had refused as "too defective," her family had learned to look past the prognosis their daughter was given: an "uncertain future." While this little girl takes seven medications a day to manage multiple challenging diagnoses, her family has been able to rejoice in her gifts. To them, she is a loving daughter and big sister, a creative, artistic, and fearless child.

Those who have completed special-needs adoption recommend that prospective parents educate themselves not only about their child's medical realities, but also about available educational resources and services. Programs like Early Intervention can be accessed more readily when contact has been established in advance. Families planning for life with a child with special needs must seek to develop strong support systems, both personal and professional. Learning how to navigate the system and identify advocates for your child before coming home will empower you to address your child's needs more effectively.

Everything God creates is good. God plans, fusses, and labors to bring about our world. He fills it with variety beyond our imaginations. Sights and sounds, smells and tastes, textures and temperatures—all our senses testify to the magnificence of creation. The divine Master Craftsman does not waste his eternity making anything substandard. Each day in that first week of creation, God looked at his work and saw goodness in all of it. We, however, may have some trouble doing that. Because we do not see things with God's eyes, we fail to appreciate the goodness—the "godness"—that encircles us.

Most people have no difficulty putting trees and animals, beaches and lakes, mountains and seasons into the plus column. There are no "deficient" flowers or "inadequate" kittens. But when we get to people, we suddenly lose that ability. There are things about ourselves and each other that we would not accept if we didn't have to. When those line items reach beyond our thresholds of tolerance, many of us reject them by rejecting the person who is attached to them. We shake our heads and shrug our shoulders, especially when we are convinced that things are not likely to improve.

There are no "perfect" children, just as there are no "perfect" parents. If your heart is open to adopting a child with serious medical or developmental challenges, you are a very special person indeed. The desire to adopt a child with special needs is an inspiration of the Holy Spirit. God, however, does not ask us to do anything that lies beyond our capabilities. Our heavenly Father gives support to what we seek within the divine will. Charity is never imprudent; but love is at times extravagant. It is that kind of over-the-top extravagant self-gift that enables the members of these special families to receive one another with thanksgiving and joy.

Holy Spirit, Author of all Good, help us to be faithful to the calling you have placed in our hearts. Guide the choices we make in our lives so that they affirm the beauty and dignity of every human life. Help us to see your image in everyone we meet. Teach us to value one another for who we

are rather than for what we are able to do. Open our hearts without fear to the weak. Empower us to love our children as they come to us and to embrace their challenges as our own. Give us great joy in small things. Seal us with both prudence and generosity that we would live within our means, but withhold nothing from you or the children who will become ours. Amen.

11
Going It Alone
Single-Parent Adoption

"In you the orphan finds mercy."
— Hosea 14:3

can't imagine raising children by myself, and yet, that is how I was raised. My parents were divorced when I was seven. My mom and I moved in with her parents after that. She worked full-time as a barber to support us. In some ways I had less than the other kids I knew, but in many ways I had more. My mother did everything within her power to provide all kinds of opportunities for me. I took music lessons, did some horseback riding, ice-skating, and gymnastics, went to camps, and attended a parochial high school. I was able to do all those things because my mother was willing to wear second-hand clothes, keep underwear with a few holes in it, and share a bedroom with me. She taught me what self-sacrifice is all about, and made me less afraid to try a little of it myself.

Single people show us that you don't have to be married to be committed to a life of love. It is not surprising, then, that more and more single people are adopting children. They are simply responding to a call they perceive in their own lives to love, to reach out, to generously give the gift of themselves.

While the ideal home in which to raise a child includes both a mother and a father, every child is better off with one loving parent than with none at all. The single mother or father can work to find ways to compensate, when possible, for the parent that is "missing." This can be done by encouraging special relationships between their adoptive children and another adult, perhaps a grandparent, godparent, or special aunt or uncle. Strong and reliable personal support systems are critical to the success of solo parenting.

The single adult contemplating adoption can gain familiarity with the ongoing demands of child raising. Volunteering to baby-sit a friend's or relative's child for more than just a few hours can give the single adult a taste of what it takes to actually parent a child. Helping to direct children's activities can also provide a way for single adults to gain familiarity with what to expect from children at various ages. Prospective parents of every marital status can benefit from realistically assessing the changes that will occur when a child enters the home. Often, these changes have more to do with altering an adult's daily routine than with such things as "childproofing" your house. Most new parents, whether their children are born to them or adopted, are not fully prepared for how little time mothers and fathers have to themselves!

Some may doubt that a single adult is able to adequately care for a child alone. The truth is that no one really parents alone. Regardless of their state in life, all parents discover sooner or later that they need help. When they do, they learn how to ask for and find it. If a single person is wholeheartedly committed to providing what a child needs, he or she will parent well. Singles, married couples, the separated and divorced, widows and widowers, and even those living a consecrated life in the Church can all be excellent parents. Of greatest importance, however, is the adoptive parent's sustained willingness to sacrifice self for the sake of the child. Time, money, expectations, and personal freedom are hardy perennials on that list of sacrifices.

As we pass through our adult lives in this world, many of us are tempted to become rather cynical. Basic fairness has become rather rare. The result is that a lot of us begin to believe that what we really want from other people is justice. All would be sunshine, I sometimes catch myself thinking, if only I got what I deserved. But when it comes right down to it, I hope for much more than I deserve. I hope for mercy. The

only place to find mercy is in God, our merciful Father and the source of all mercy. If mercy is what we seek, we can be sure to find it with him.

The single life offers a unique image of the merciful presence of God. While singles may feel like a fifth wheel at times, God has no less a plan for their lives than for the lives of married couples. Single adults have a degree of personal freedom that can enable them to make their lives a radical gift of service in love. They are often the ones who fill in the gaps, who are available in a pinch, who are willing and able to step into the breach when no one else can or will. Many times a single friend of ours has offered to help one of our kids with something I either couldn't do, or just didn't have time for.

All of us are able to pass on to others what we have received from God. The Holy Spirit inspires us to obtain mercy by acting mercifully. When we do this, we transform the world into a place where people can encounter God's loving kindness in one another. Many of us practice the works of mercy—both corporal and spiritual—right in our own homes. Every day parents clothe the naked, feed the hungry, instruct the ignorant, and admonish little sinners who, at times, commit not-so-little sins! Family life and love demands that each member treat all the others with mercy.

If you are a single person seeking a way to live a life of love and self-gift, adopting a child is a beautiful way to do it. Every child deserves a loving family; not every child has one. Somewhere in the world there is a child who is alone. The great injustice of that loneliness can be healed by an act of mercy. Your willingness to give your life to a child in need makes the world a more merciful place for us all.

Holy Spirit, Spirit of Counsel and Fortitude, I come to you with a willingness to serve. I have heard your call to make myself a total gift. Now I ask you to show me how and to whom I should give myself. Strengthen my commitment to love not only in theory, but in daily reality. Teach me to embrace self-sacrifice with joy, to give freely all that I am and have. Direct me to those whose support I will need, and give me the grace to ask for help and to receive it. Bless the children you have called me to love with the richness of mercy you have inspired in me. Amen.

12

The Paper Pregnancy
Getting Your Dossier Together

> ...If every one of them were written down, I
> suppose that the world itself could not con-
> tain the books that would be written.
> — John 21:25b

$\mathcal{T}$he process of adoption turned me into a mail-
box watcher. Every day, as soon as I saw that flag go up,
I'd run outside to get the mail. I was always expecting
something. When the thick envelope of blank forms to
fill out came from our agency, I was delighted. Looking
at the dossier checklist, I felt like a racehorse just
released from the gate, ready to run hard to the finish.
Like everyone who seeks to adopt a child, I wanted it all
done yesterday. The volume of what was required, however, forced me to take a slower pace. With so many
people to contact, so many annoying little obstacles to

overcome, and so many details to keep track of, I had to find a sensible rhythm to the process.

I began to realize that if I were going to get through it all, I would have to do so with diligence and discipline, not anxious compulsion. That would not be easy for me. Andrew had a different dragon to battle: a tendency toward procrastination. We were able to make steady progress, however, when I let go of unrealistic expectations and demands, and when he kept the ball rolling. No longer looking at the whole of what had to be done, we started taking it one piece at a time. The key was to do something every day, rather than trying to do everything at once. We stuck with it even when it felt as if we were chipping away at Mount Everest with an ice pick. Our dossier was complete in about two months.

Biological parents float along their way with very little paperwork. Adoptive parents find themselves swimming—hopefully not drowning!—in it. The sheer volume of information that must be gathered and submitted is substantial and can seem overwhelming. Among the requirements: marriage license, medical information, financial data, criminal records, deeds to property, letters of recommendation, personal statements, and endless forms of every imaginable kind expressly certifying every imaginable thing. Prospective parents compile an album including photographs of themselves, their family, and every room of their house. Holiday celebrations, the kind of town you live in, and the distance from your home to the closest hospital are just some of the data points prospective parents must collect and present. All documents must be individually notarized. I considered becoming a notary public myself just to make things easier, but then I found out a notary cannot certify her own signature. Suffice it to say that by the time our paperwork was done, we knew the location and hours of just about every notary within striking distance.

For those adopting internationally, there are the added joys of immigration clearance, citizenship applications, and an official fingerprinting of all adults living in the household. It was a bit strange to take my 87-year-old grandmother for fingerprinting—even stranger when she told the government official it was for an international adoption! All submitted information must then be translated. In addition to notarization, each separate document going overseas must also receive a special seal called an *apostille*. (I had always thought there were twelve, but we ended up with well over 100!) Apostilles are obtained from the office of the Secretary of State in which the document originated. If you were born in Ohio and your spouse was born in Idaho, the two of you married in Virginia, but now live in New Hampshire, you will be sending documents to four different states for international apostilles. Some charge two or three dollars apiece; in other states the fees can be as much as twenty dollars each.

The mass of paper that results from all this flurry—properly collated, of course—is the dossier. Getting it done can be rather stressful. Dotting every "i" and crossing every "t" is a monumental and lengthy process. There is always a small subset of papers, too, that may expire before the adoption is completed. Those must be redone and submitted again. To anyone actively engaged in the process, it seems as if there is no end to what must be assembled. Those who make the mistake of thinking that adoption is less involved than biological childbearing soon find that their lives can be comparably dominated by pregnancy's paper equivalent.

All adoptive parents know how easy it is to get caught up in the excitement of adopting a child. What they may not know is that it is almost as easy to get tripped up by the intricacies involved. Parents who recognize that adoption has its own process and timetable are already ahead of the game. Those who try to exercise control are likely to experience a great deal of unnecessary frustration and anxiety. It is wiser to give yourself over to the process than it is to fight it. Swimming frantically against the current does not result in a faster adoption or a "better" child. On the other hand, a prospective parent who procrastinates will not be able to accomplish what needs to be done. Neither laziness nor obsessiveness offers much assistance for the task at hand. Setting realistic goals and deadlines is what helped us complete what we had to do.

There is more to history than anyone can learn from reading a book. Even those who read all that has been written on a subject do not end up knowing all there is to know. Life is bigger than what we can fit onto a page, or even thousands of pages. Paper and life are not well matched, for while the page begins empty, our lives start off filled beyond the margins.

Writing a personal resume or college application brings this challenge into focus. If we find it difficult to put our experiences into words, we will discover that it is even harder to communicate our identity on paper. Hopefully, what we do is an expression of who we are, a window into what is at the heart of us. But as we go deeper, we cannot help but wonder whether our inner beings have a lot less to do with what is at the surface than we once thought. Growing in experience we learn that people are far more than what they seem to be on paper. Sometimes, they are very different from what can be written about them.

Jesus lived a relatively short life on earth. So much happened during the three years of his public ministry, however, that John ends his Gospel by telling us that not even all the libraries in all the world could hold what it would take to record everything Jesus did. The Gospel writers had to pick and choose. They could not tell it all. More than communicating what Jesus did, their stories were meant to tell who Jesus was. The choices each one made in the telling also reveal something about themselves.

When you begin to wade through the paperwork, the end will not be in sight, but there will be an end to the process you are pursuing. Those who stay the course finish it in time. You may not know how long the road is, but the one you are traveling will lead you to a child. Love perseveres. What it takes to assemble your dossier is just a taste of the persistent love that will come to permeate your family life. It is the love that conquers, the love by which we become the children of God.

Holy Spirit, Spirit of Perseverance, help us to do what must be done. Protect us from anxiety and doubt. Keep our eyes on what lies beyond the task, and guide us through each step with diligence. Guard our hearts from the desire to control. Defend our souls from discouragement. Comfort us when we are tired and overwhelmed. Gently show us the truth about ourselves, and give us the grace to tell that truth without fear. Help us to finish what has been set before us. Watch over our children as we do what is necessary to bring them home. Amen.

13

The Waiting Parent
Making Patient Preparations

"Do not let your hearts be troubled. Believe in God, believe also in me. In my father's house there are many dwelling places. If it were not so, would I have told you that I go to prepare a place for you? And if I go and prepare a place for you, I will come again and will take you to myself, so that where I am, there you may be also."

— John 14:1–3

Things should have settled down when all of our paperwork was done, but they didn't simply because I couldn't. For some reason, no longer having a stack of things to do made me nervous and compulsive. I became anxious about almost everything to do with our plan to adopt. Questions flooded my mind all day long, and even kept me up at night. When were we going to hear something? Where would we be sent? What would we find when we got there? Were we doing the right thing? Impatience grew as I allowed myself to be consumed by the desire to *know*. All that inner churning, however, prevented me from making genuine preparations. The waiting could have been joyful. Instead, it was aggravating.

Andrew and I handled the waiting very differently. His strategy was to focus on everything else in our lives. Mine was to research every possibility I could imagine. While Andrew didn't see much point in discussing hypotheticals, I couldn't pay attention to much else. My severe case of "are-we-there-yet" found a positive outlet when I discovered active adoption communities on the internet. Some groups were devoted to adoptions from certain countries, others centered on children of a certain age group, or with particular needs. People at every stage in the adoption process were ready and willing to share from the treasury of their experiences.

Adoptions have no due date. Strangely, though, there seems to be a clock that starts ticking inside us as soon as we initiate the process to adopt. Taking each step as it comes, there are times when everything seems to move at the speed of light. There are also quiet periods lasting weeks or even months, times when it appears that nothing is happening. The flurry of activity may overwhelm us. The quiet, however, challenges us to accept the fact that we are not in control.

Holding patiently onto hope is not as simple as it sounds. People who have waited several years to have a child often fear yet another disappointment. Others may not fully appreciate the twists and turns inherent in the adoption process. Ultimately, however, we must come to the point of making a decision to trust the Spirit who first prompted us to complete what he started. We are able to do so when we can place our time into the context of God's eternity.

While we may not feel that waiting furthers the adoption process, in truth, it serves the adopting family well. Waiting gives you time for real preparation. It is a sabbatical for both learning and rest. Having few active items on your to-do list provides an opportunity to reflect and to plan. The time you spend waiting can be profitable if you make good use of it. Rooms can be set up. Schools can be contacted. Advice can be sought out. All the necessary parental accessories can be purchased—and assembled. Even more, you will have the luxury of being able to sort through all that you are feeling. Rest, reflect, and enjoy one another while you are still able to do so freely. Once your child arrives home, you may have far less time for those things than you might expect.

Nothing is more difficult than waiting. Whether we anticipate the future with joy or dread, there is something deep in human nature that resists—even resents—having to wait. We find the interim an intolerable place to be. Some of us fidget our days away with frenetic activity. Others become apathetic toward their own lives. Personally, I'm more the frenetic type.

The world we live in is not exactly conducive to patience. Express lines, microwaves, fast food: our society places a very high value on speed and convenience. It seems, however, that even though we can get what we want faster than ever, we find it increasingly difficult to remain hopeful. In truth, patience and hope are related. If one is missing, chances are that the other will not be found either.

We tend to talk about hope as if it were some kind of vain wish. We hope for good weather. We hope the waitress comes to take our order soon. We hope that our team wins the game. The Scriptures paint a very different picture. Hope is not something we wish for. Hope is something we expectantly wait for. When we wish, it is because we cannot bring about whatever we are wishing for. Hope, however, belongs to those who have done everything they can do. Hope is not passive. It is the act of trusting God to bring about what we desire according to the divine will.

When we trust, we are able to wait patiently. Knowing that something good will come, we are content to have something to look forward to. Patience is the fruit of that conviction. It rises with hope in the hearts of those who believe what they do not see. Impatience, on the other hand, is rooted in the desire to control. Those who find it difficult to trust that things will turn out for the best tend toward panic. Often rushing into the middle of a situation, they intervene more from desperation than from vision. In the end, they may not even realize that all they ever really needed to do was wait.

God is always preparing us. There is not a day that goes by or a lesson we have learned that God will not eventually use for our benefit. Those piano lessons you took as a child, the time you helped your father fix the shingles on the roof, the demanding eighth grade English teacher nobody liked, the loser you are embarrassed to admit you ever dated: every experience of our lives can be a divine preparation. The heavenly Father is ever working in each one of us, making us ready to receive him and one another. The deepest preparations are those made in the heart. God does not plant seeds in untilled soil.

Our Lord prepares us, but he also prepares things for us. The Holy Spirit is the divine Trailblazer, making a path for us to travel where there was none before. The Spirit guides us along the way that leads to all that God has promised us. That is no small thing, for the Lord is busy creating a place for each and every person. We do not need to worry about being left out in the cold. There is no reason to allow our hearts to be troubled, for God is worthy of our trust.

Holy Spirit, Spirit of Patience and Peace, teach us how to wait joyfully in hope. Calm our hearts and minds. Keep us from frenzy and guard us from apathy. Help us to rest in confidence and to be grateful for the time you have given us to prepare our homes. Show us how to make the deeper preparations, to ready our hearts—and not just our houses—to receive the children you will give us. Inspire us to trust you and to entrust ourselves and our children to your care. Fill our days and nights with your peace. And lead us all to the place you are preparing for us to dwell with you forever. Amen.

14

Ready or Not!
Getting "the Call"

But when the fullness of time had come, God sent his son born of a woman, born under the law, in order to redeem those who were under the law, so that we might receive adoption as children. And because you are children, God has sent the Spirit of his Son into our hearts, crying "Abba! Father!" So you are no longer a slave, but a child, and if a child, then also an heir, through God.

— Galatians 4:4–7

$\mathcal{S}$omewhere during our adoption process, it occurred to me that timing was the single most influentially factor in determining what child would ultimately become ours. In our family's case, that turned out to be true in spades. The child we adopted was almost

completely determined by when we were told to book our trip.

We had hoped to travel during a week of winter school vacation, but as things progressed, it did not seem that would work out. Suddenly, however, all the necessary pieces lined up. Our paperwork had made it overseas, and we were able to book the first of our two trips to Russia in February, as we had hoped. Our call to fly came suddenly. While I was thrilled by the prospect of finding our daughter, I admit to feeling a bit apprehensive about how quickly things seemed to be moving. Suddenly, waiting seemed safe! Andrew was concerned that we would feel very ambivalent toward the child we would ultimately choose. We both wondered how we would know what to do. I think both of us worried a little about what would happen if the two of us didn't agree. Because everyone we knew was full of excitement, we didn't exactly feel as though we could share our apprehensions.

No one wanted to run through the process faster than I. But when the call came, I had the inner sense of being rushed. It was not until much later on that we realized why everything had to move as quickly as it did. God's plan for us became clear in the fullness of time.

During that first trip, we met a number of children; one of them was our daughter. Later on we were told that if we had traveled three months later, our little girl would not have been at the orphanage we visited. Around the time of her third birthday in May, she would have been moved out of the "baby house" to a facility for older children. Because we had requested an infant, we would never have met her. Similarly, if we had decided to adopt a year earlier, we would not have been sent to our daughter's region. Voronezh had been legally closed to international adoption for a period of nearly two years. Either earlier or later and we would have adopted a different child. Our daughter would not have become ours.

Every adopting parent runs to the phone when it rings, hoping to receive that long-awaited call from the adoption agency. But when that call does come, it is normal to feel a bit uncertain about what you are undertaking. Adopting a child is serious business. The closer to reality it becomes, the more you begin to realize just how serious it is. Climbing the mountain of paperwork and preparations is arduous; reaching the peak is exhilarating. But when the ball starts rolling down the hill, most adoptive parents find they aren't nearly as ready as they thought they were. Some may feel as if the process they initiated is destined to run them over. I sure did!

You may have waited for years, months, or weeks to hear the news that you would soon meet your new son or daughter. Likely, you will have had all your ducks in a row well in advance of receiving that much anticipated phone call. All you will need to do when the phone rings is answer it. Go gently forward. No one will force you to take a step you do not feel good about. No child is ever adopted accidentally. You will have all the time you need, definitely not less, probably not more.

Life is not a stream of random events punctuated by a few coincidences. Both darkness and light stretch across our lives, connecting and highlighting one another. Together, they create a coherent whole that is more than the sum of individual happenings.

Looking back, every one of us can see emerging patterns and themes in events that were not apparent to us at the time. Characters come and go. They themselves evolve and all the while they transform us. Events, both positive and negative, shape us by how we respond to them. In turn, our actions influence the lives of others.

We have all witnessed instances in which events are mysteriously drawn together and things fall into place. That is the essence of what the Scriptures call "the fullness of time." Time rarely reaches its fullness when we expect or want it to. But when the moment arrives, there is nothing that we can do to stop or delay it. God moves when we have finished taking our turn. When he does, however, it often feels as if we are suddenly playing a different game.

Faith teaches us that God is personally involved in human affairs. God is not merely our Creator, but our

Father. Our lives have a purpose and a goal. The divine will works in, through, and around us to bring about the fullness of who we are and why we are. We do not need to wonder if we are in the right place at the right time. If we are in God's hands, we are never anywhere else.

The Holy Spirit works precisely on schedule. Nobody has a better sense of timing than the Eternal One. God will bring together everything that is necessary just when it is necessary. When all the relevant people are in their proper places, just remember to hang on! Your hat may fly off your head; your stomach may feel a bit queasy; you might even let out a scream as you plunge into the thrill and adventure of family life. But oh, what a joyous ride it is!

Holy Spirit, Finger of God, help us to see your presence in the process and to trust that things will unfold according to your will. Maker of divine appointments, bring us to the right place at the right time. Give us the grace to wait for the fullness of time and the wisdom to recognize that moment when it comes. Teach us to place our lives in your hands. Prepare us to receive what we have asked for. Prepare our children to receive us too. Give them hope and the reassurance of your embrace until that day when we share your warmth together. Amen.

15

Your Child?

Search and Referral

You are children of the LORD your God. For you are a people holy to the LORD your God; it is you the LORD has chosen out of all the peoples on earth to be his people, his treasured possession.

— Deuteronomy 14:1a, 2

*P*art of what attracted us to the adoption agency we chose was that we could travel to Russia "blind," that is, without a referral to a specific child. The process we felt most comfortable with involved visiting a few orphanages in order to find a child who was right for us. Many people warned us that if we searched for our daughter ourselves, we would end up wanting to adopt every child we met. That was not our experience, however.

Excitement and jet lag don't mix very well. The combination kept me awake most of our first night in Moscow. We knew where we were going and what we were looking for; we just weren't too sure what we would find. Flying in a propeller plane to Voronezh the following afternoon, everything we saw through the window looked black and white. The region is part of what is known as *"chernozemny,"* or black earth. Covered in snow and leafless birch trees, the Russian winter lived up to its reputation.

When we landed at the airport, we were met by our adoption facilitator, Oleg, and a professional translator. They took us directly to the first orphanage we were scheduled to visit. Alla, a neuropathologist and the director of the "baby house," greeted us in her office. Arrayed in a formal chiffon gown and lab coat, she was, to say the least, colorfully eccentric. Her appearance was a bit startling, and so were her first words: darting her eyes between us intently, she told us, "I have a little girl here who looks just like you!"

The facility was immaculate and orderly. We were happy to see that someone had taken the time to paint Russian fairy tale characters on the hallway walls. Pulling us aside on the way up the stairs, our translator, Renata, told us that it was standard procedure for an orphanage to have prospective parents meet a few of the older children first. While most families intend to adopt a baby, she explained, orphanage staffs were anxious to give their toddlers a chance to find a home before they graduated to the next level of the system. She instructed us to be polite with the children, but to remain firm in our desire to adopt a child between one and two years old.

The second floor room was large and bright with wood paneled walls, large windows, and the wildly intricate parquet flooring we saw almost everywhere in Russia. A large number of hand-painted child sized chairs arched around the outer wall. An old upright piano was placed near the center of the long wall, and a little plastic slide was pushed into a corner. On one end of the room were words posted in large cut-out Cyrillic letters. They said something about "peace." Suddenly, we heard Alla's voice in the hallway, and the sound of little feet.

Masha was the first child we met. Her short brown hair was very fine. Exceptionally small for her age, it was hard to believe that she was almost three. Masha looked so much like us and our other children that our facilitator jokingly asked Andrew if he was sure that he had not been in Russia before! Entering the room, Masha did whatever the director told her to do. She sat down, stood up, greeted us, and did a little dance. When she stretched her red and black velour dress out to twirl, I noticed that she was wearing boys' underwear.

A child psychologist was brought in to explain Masha's background. Her full name was Maria. She had been placed in the orphanage at nine months of age due to parental neglect. A bit more information about her birth mother was offered, as well as her medical history and health record. The psychologist commented that Masha was considered a social child, playing well with other children. Evidently, she had a mind of her own too, in that she refused to eat foods she didn't like. That was quite an assertion of self for an orphan who did not have enough food to begin with!

Masha's lively brown eyes sparkled with interest. I had the feeling that she had done this routine before, and that at some level she knew what it was all about. This proved to be true: months later, after we brought Masha home, she told me she had met other families who didn't want to take her home.

Two other little girls about the same age joined us. We had brought some toys along and passed them around to the girls. One of them, Valentina, seemed to have obvious developmental delays. She was interested only in the rattle. The other, a beautiful blonde named Olga, seemed timid, and sat rather passively on her caretaker's lap. We were told that she had been sent to Moscow for surgery to correct a congenital heart condition. Masha, however, picked up the musical stuffed animal we'd brought and danced with it; figuring out how to make it sing took her no time at all.

Masha exuded personality much as our other children do, and was completely enchanted by a small photo book of our family. Watching her play, I began to imagine how well she would fit into our family. Suddenly, I realized that we had a serious problem on our hands. Masha was the "right" child, but the "wrong" age. She was not the "baby on the other side of the world" we had been praying for—or was she? When it was time for her to leave the room, she asked the director if she could keep the toy and book. Our answer was an uncomfortable "no." We had brought those items as gifts for our daughter. We were not yet sure that we had found her. Without any further discussion, Masha left smiling.

Not giving up on our well-thought-out plan to adopt a younger child, we visited another orphanage the following day. There we met an absolutely beautiful eleven-month-old girl named Anastasia. She was exactly the kind of child we had hoped to find—the right age, the right gender, the right background, even one of my favorite names. Anastasia was so terrified of us, however, that all she did when I held her was cry. My husband had only to look in her direction, and she burst into tears. Baby Anastasia was everything we thought we wanted, but when it came down to it, she was clearly someone else's daughter. Even though we visited her a second day, neither one of us felt that she was meant for us.

It took us three days to get our heads around adopting a child who would be five months older than our

youngest daughter. We tried to consider every facet of
what bringing home a three-year-old would mean.
During that time we worked through the issues with
the rest of our family via e-mail and digital photographs. On the very last day, we called home and spoke
with each one of them. Some of our children argued
for sticking with the original plan to bring home a
baby. Others were excited by the prospect of having
more in common with a somewhat older child. All of
them were primarily concerned with how their youngest sister would be affected by the decision.

Together, we came to the conclusion that Masha
was God's plan for us—or perhaps more accurately, that
we were God's plan for Masha. The Holy Spirit had
brought us to Russia to find her. By the time we signed
our intention to adopt, we had spent almost six hours
with her. At the end of our last visit, we gave Masha the
musical toy and the photo book with all our names written in Russian as our pledge to come back at the next
available court date and take her home. We also signed
the orphanage referral book, and filed our choice to
adopt Masha with the Ministry of Education.

In the adoption process, once all the paperwork is
done, the next step is ordinarily the referral. We traveled "blind" to find our own "referral." Usually, however, an agency calls when an individual child has been
matched to prospective parents by those who are responsible for the child's care. Often a photo or video is pro-

vided, along with some medical information and the personal history of the child. It is not uncommon, though, for parents to be instructed to travel to meet their referred child with little advance information. In other situations, the child available for adoption may not yet have been born. Adoptive parents may be asked to meet an expectant birth mother. Then too, there are parents who receive an emergency call from a local department of child services. However it is that the match is made, both prospective and birth parents have decisions to make. Those decisions, which until this point have been rather abstract and general, suddenly become both specific and personal.

Adopting a child is not like shopping in a department store. People, after all, are not made to order. There is a certain need for flexibility in families seeking to adopt a new member. Parents should have a sense of what they would be willing to accept that is different from what they originally hoped for in a child. A smooth referral process depends on your ability to know your limits and live within them. Distinguishing between negotiables and non-negotiables with respect to race, gender, health, and age enables adopting parents greater flexibility in accepting a referral. God is in the business of adopting the whole human race. We, however, have a few more limitations!

Some parents feel compelled—for all kinds of reasons—to reject an adoption referral. When we committed ourselves to adopting Masha, we chose not to adopt Olga, Anastasia, or Valentina. Accepting one child made it necessary for us to decide against adopting all the other children who deserved a home and family just as much as Masha. That difficult decision should be met with understanding and not judgment. Because adoption becomes very personal when you commit your life to an individual child, the decision to do so must be made with more certainty than apprehension. Every successful adoption is motivated by love, not guilt. The choice to adopt a particular child must be fully informed and fully free.

From the outside, the process of search and referral may seem rather cruel. The sad reality is that some children will be left behind. Referral, however, is not a means to determine which children a family will reject. It is the procedural vehicle to identify the child a family will choose to love for the rest of their lives. Parents cannot adopt all the children they see. They need only find the one to whom their hearts speak a resounding "yes."

Every family hoping to adopt has the same question. How do you know when you've found your child? The truth is that you may not know at all. Prospective parents must listen carefully to their hearts. After all is said and done, adoption is an act of faith.

We all bear the image of God, but Baptism makes us children of God in Christ, in a new dimension of grace. It effects a change in us. Each one of us has a destiny, something toward which we are headed. While our paths are unique, the place we are meant to arrive at is shared. The heavenly Father searches the world for us. The God who made us all calls us forward to himself. We are not chosen for God alone. By God, we are also chosen for one another. Our Father intends for us to be one family.

The process of our spiritual adoption is divinely initiated. Through adoption Israel belongs to God, and Christians are called children of the Most High. While we may cooperate with the grace we receive, that grace does not originate in us. Grace comes to us through God's only Son. The life, death, and resurrection of Jesus empowers us to become members of the eternal household of heaven. God never wonders whether we are meant to be his. We are created for the Creator. We are God's treasure, destined and chosen to belong.

God's work doesn't stop at the boundary between the spiritual and the concrete. The Holy Spirit is active in every realm of existence. We may think that our plan to adopt was our own bright idea. But in reality, only God can claim complete credit for it. Adopting families are inspired by the Holy Spirit. Just as God created marriage and the family, God also "invented" adoption.

Holy Spirit, Spirit of Joy, speak to our hearts. Keep our hearts open to all the children we meet. Guide us in interpreting what we see. Lead us to the children you have promised us. Give us wisdom to discern the information we receive. Help us to balance our expectations with the realities we encounter. Fill us with confidence in the choices we make, and teach us to walk by faith with joy. Help us to know your will for us and for the children with whom we will share life. Comfort any fears our children may have. Bless them with the same joy you have given us. Amen.

16
Pink or Blue?
The Gender Option

May our sons in their youth be like plants full
grown, our daughters like corner pillars, cut
for the building of a palace.

— Psalm 144:12

We decided to request a little girl very early in
formulating our plan to adopt. Our reasoning was simply
a matter of balance. Because our youngest daughter was
preceded by two older brothers, and because the next sister up the ladder was seven years older, we thought it
would be best to add more pink to the mix. Intentionally
surrounding our youngest daughter with brothers was
not something that seemed particularly appealing—or
fair. From our point of view, she needed a sister.

Our daughters, of course, were thrilled; our sons,
less so. They had hoped that our plan to adopt would

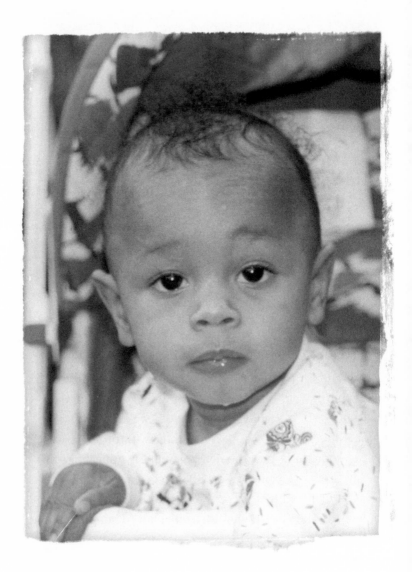

help them to get even, that is, balance our family's ratio of boys to girls. Accepting our rationale, however, they resigned themselves to a final score of boys: 3, girls: 5. In the end, they recognized that the choice was not nearly as important for them as it was for their youngest sister.

All parents dream about their future children. When we do, we imagine them looking and acting in particular ways. Generally, the pictures we paint in our minds reflect our personal preferences. It is not uncommon for us to project of bit of ourselves onto what we imagine about our children. If we have brown curls or blue eyes, chances are that the children we dream up do, too. If we are athletes or passionate readers, outgoing or reserved, we will tend to imagine our children sharing those interests and traits. Gender preferences often shape the mental images we create. Many mothers happily anticipate dressing up their little girls in velvet with ruffly tights and black patent leather shoes. More than a few fathers, on the other hand, are just as eager to imagine fishing or playing catch with their sons. When I think about it, before I had children I pictured them all as golden-haired girls with green eyes and larger-than-average noses running barefoot through fields of tall grass. Not one of our eight fits that description—except, of course, for the bare feet.

The relationships our families share and build are influenced, but not determined, by gender. Mothers and daughters have a different kind of relationship than do mothers and sons. Likewise, the dynamic between fathers and sons is quite distinct from what develops between fathers and their daughters. I can attest from experience that brothers and sisters deal with each other in ways as different as night and day.

Gender is one of the choices adoptive parents can make but birth parents cannot. Being able to exercise an option, however, doesn't necessarily mean that it is best to do so. There are many reasons to adopt a boy, and an equal number of reasons to adopt a girl. Ultimately, prospective parents must decide whether they have a good reason to choose either. Numerous adoptive families choose to remain open to either a boy or a girl.

That being said, there is nothing wrong with choosing the gender of the child you will adopt. People do exercise the gender option for all kinds of reasons. Some, having fond memories of an older brother, choose to adopt a boy first. Others believe that they will be better prepared to raise a daughter than a son—or the opposite. Families with tight living quarters may select one gender over another so that their children can share a room.

The most important consideration regarding the gender of your adopted child is determining just how important having a son or daughter is. Gender is an area in which a family is able to allow a degree of flexibility. The path, while broad at the beginning, must eventually narrow toward a commitment to a particular child. Selecting the gender of a child—or refusing to do so—will lead parents down one fork in the road ahead.

Whether our children are boys or girls—or boys *and* girls!—we want to see all of them reach their potential. Every parent looks for areas in which our children excel. We readily notice that a child can catch a ball or sing on pitch. It may be more challenging to identify the portion of every child's giftedness that lies hidden in his or her gender. While our culture accepts that both boys and girls can grow up to be firefighters or teachers, we sometimes overlook the things that belong to us simply because we are male or female. These attributes flow from the essence of who we are and not what we do. A girl may grow up to be an excellent mother, and a boy may become a caring father. These roles are not interchangeable. They are complementary by design. God intends them to be so.

While both have attempted to do so, neither gender can claim divine preference. The Scriptures are full of godly men and godly women. Although Biblical cultures were largely patriarchal, there are plentiful stories celebrating women for their heroism and holiness. Some—like Deborah and Esther—exercised leadership in the community, while others found their vocations in other less visible roles. The same can be said of men of God.

There is nothing haphazard about how we are created. We are intended to be exactly who we are. There are no assembly lines in heaven, no conveyor belts on which souls are randomly injected into bodies. God has a plan for every single one of us. It is with that plan in mind that each of us is made.

Everything we need to fulfill God's unique purpose for our lives is built into who we are. Our Creator equips each one of us to become what he designed us to be. Masculinity or femininity is part of how God does that. At the beginning of creation, God designed humanity to be male and female. Thus, from our very origins we express a divinely given complementarity. Men and women together bear the image of God. God indeed loves all his children, both sons and daughters. Masculine and feminine, the Lord delights in us all.

Holy Spirit, Gift of the Most High, teach us to recognize the beauty of all that you have given us. Help us to rejoice not only in similarities, but in differences. Give us a true appreciation for your call to us as men and as women. Dispel our suspicions. Enlighten our minds. Dispose our hearts toward one another in love. Heal the hurts we may have suffered in unhealthy relationships, as well as those we may have caused to others. Show us how to embrace our children fully as the sons and daughters you have given us. Keep us always close to the heavenly Father we share and in whose image we were created. Amen.

17

How Old Are You?
Age and Birth Order

If any of you is lacking in wisdom, ask God, who gives to all generously and ungrudgingly, and it will be given you.

— James 1:5

$\mathcal{T}$he most confounding aspect of our adoption process involved our daughter's age. Meeting Masha suddenly made everything difficult and confusing. She didn't look much like the "baby" we had planned to adopt, nor did she match our homestudy's description of an "infant child from Russia." While we were pretty convinced that Masha was the "right" child for us, she was older than any child we had envisioned adopting.

None of our options seemed very good to us at the time. While we didn't feel right about continuing to search for a younger child, we were very unsure about committing ourselves to a virtual three-year-old. Masha did not appear to have any of the issues we were afraid of in an "older" child. Other than her size, she didn't seem too far behind a normal developmental schedule. Masha didn't seem to be angry or aggressive; neither was she lethargic. When we spoke to her, she made direct eye contact and did her best to understand and respond.

Still, we were concerned about her ability to adjust to life outside of an institution, as well as about how our youngest daughter would feel about having an instant "twin." Resisting the inclination to decide and move on, we asked God to make his will clear to us. After a few days—and a whole lot of e-mail traffic back and forth from home—we became quite convinced that Masha was meant to be our daughter. In the end, our choice was between choosing the "right" age or the "right" child. Our youngest daughter would hold her position at the end of the line. Without knowing it, we already had our "baby."

In retrospect, I don't know why we struggled over Masha's age as much as we did. Our two little girls are very close. They are always thinking about each other. When one asks for a cookie, she always makes sure to get one for her sister too. People often ask if our girls are twins. I'm never quite sure how to answer. If I'm feeling impish, I say no, tell them that the girls are five months apart, and leave it at that. Watching them try to figure it out can be rather amusing!

Age plays a larger role in adoption than one might guess. It is one of the first dominos in a long sequence of cause and effect that is relevant to much that an adoptive family will address in time. Health, development, emotional well-being, and the dynamics of family relationships can all be influenced by a child's age at adoption.

Age is an important piece of information in evaluating a child's health, partly because there are several medical conditions that cannot be recognized in young infants. Autism, for example, is not often diagnosed until a child is between eighteen and twenty-four months. Developmental milestones are similarly age-related. Speech and language difficulties are not likely to be noticed until a child is two or three. Furthermore, the care a child is receiving may make it difficult to tell the difference between temporary developmental delays and long-term disabilities. Post-institutional children present a unique set of challenges in this area. Adoption experts claim that for every three months a child spends in an orphanage, there is one month of developmental delay.

Emotional issues, too, are influenced by a child's age. While adoption is in the long-term best interest of a child, it is an enormous adjustment—at times, even traumatic. The tools a child has to make those adjustments are largely determined by his or her level of development. A baby, for example, has neither the

language skills nor the cognitive ability to express emotions in a clear or intelligible way. An older child is able
to identify and express feelings. Bonding with an infant
is quite different from bonding with a toddler or
school-aged child. Age may also be a factor in how, later
in life, a child will address having been adopted.
Children brought home during infancy have no living
memory of a personal past before adoption. While
some parents may consider this an advantage, there are
children who do not. The inability to connect to the
past can become a recurring theme in some children's
lives. Slightly older children may remember their birth
parents or orphanage life in detail. For some of them,
the memories are comforting; for others, they are a
source of fear and insecurity.

A child's age at the time of adoption may also influence how a family's children relate to one another.
Adoption makes it possible to bring an older brother or
sister into the mix, or place a new child between children already in the home. Issues such as sibling rivalry
are often directly affected by birth order.

To choose a child's age is essentially to make a
choice between "history" and "mystery." On one hand,
an infant may appear to present adoptive parents with
more of a "blank slate," that is, less of a past to contend
with. But a baby may also bring unrevealed challenges
that parents did not expect to address. In contrast, an
older child has a past that should not—and really can-

not—be ignored. Older children need parents who are committed to taking over where others left off, and adding in what others left out. When a child has more of a "past," the effects of that past are often more visible. The most difficult part of making a choice about age is the lack of information about how any choice might play out. Adoptive parents cannot know everything we wish we did.

People have never been as well educated as they are today. World literacy is at its highest level in human history. We know more than we ever did, and the volume of what there is to know is outpacing our ability to learn it. As a result, the number of years we spend in school continues to increase. Today, our children learn considerably more than their grandparents did, and at a much younger age. Why is it, then, that people who know so much more don't seem to be any smarter?

We aren't as bright as we think we are because we need something more—something other than mere knowledge. We need wisdom. Formal education can teach us knowledge that informs. But wisdom is the power to know if, when, and how to use the knowledge we have gained. Wisdom helps us discern what is genuinely important.

Wise people exercise what used to be called "good judgment." The notion of good judgment implies that there is such a thing as bad judgment. It also, however, stands against the popular misconception that judgment in and of itself is "bad." As much as we try to avoid it, our lives are full of decisions. We can hope that the decisions we make are based on something more substantial that what we ate for breakfast. Ultimately, the values we hold and the principles we maintain guide us in the decisions—or judgments—we make every day. We are wise when we do more than just live. Wisdom is knowing how to live.

There are times in life when no decision seems right or good. There are also times when every option we have appears equally beneficial. Those kinds of situations often offer an opportunity for us to grow wise. Human life is full of confusion and uncertainty. We have all experienced times in which we truly had no idea what we should do. Lacking wisdom, however, is no cause for worry. When we don't know what to do, all we have to do is ask God for help. Our all-knowing and all-wise Father will give us wisdom. Notice, though, that the Lord does not promise us the wisdom we need—but only the wisdom we ask for. God wants us to *ask.*

In truth, no child is a completely fresh canvas, but no child's future is totally determined by her past. Your child's age comes as a package of both challenges and gifts. There are parents who are happy to skip the diapers and potty training stages when adopting a child. There are also parents who (don't ask me why!) would consider their lives somehow incomplete without the diapers. Some choose to adopt when older children are grown. Others adopt an older brother or sister for children they already have. The unknowns of adopting an infant may be a bit frightening; the difficult past bound to an older child may seem daunting. Somehow, however, the challenges of both history and mystery fade in the eyes of a child who has waited—however long—for loving parents.

Holy Spirit, Spirit of Wisdom, you know all that has passed and all that will be. Guide us along the path you desire us to take. Give us the wisdom we need and the courage to ask for it when we need it. Help us to discern what is right for our family. Keep us from carrying what is too heavy for us. Teach us to commend everything and everyone into your hands. Reassure us in what we do not or cannot know. Sustain us in all that we do know, but do not have the power to change. Fill us with gratitude for the gifts you have given our children, as well as for the challenges that accompany those gifts. Bless the children you have chosen to be ours, and make us a blessing to them for the rest of their lives. Amen.

18

Add or Multiply?
Adopting More Than One at a Time

"May God almighty bless you and make you fruitful and numerous, that you may become a company of peoples."

— Genesis 28:3

$\mathcal{B}$efore we traveled to Russia, a few of our friends predicted that when we met the children at the orphanages we would want to take them all home. They probably figured that after having seven kids, we would hardly notice a few more! Even our adoption agency and homestudy worker suggested that we request immigration approval for two or even three children. Politely declining, we determined that the best thing for us was to take on adoption the same way we had taken on birth—one at a time. Locking in to an approval for only one child was a kind of insurance policy against an emotionally driven desire to rescue more children than we were truly prepared to handle.

Having never encountered children living in an institutional setting, I was somewhat concerned about how I would feel, or more accurately, how I would be able to handle the high tide of emotion I anticipated. We already knew that the children did not have enough food to eat, that their lives were completely regimented and without freedom, that the orphanage workers did not have the time or resources to give individual attention to any child. Knowledge, however, can be rather different from experience. Actually seeing how these children lived first-hand was certain to evoke a compassion in us. Compassion, after all, was one of the things that drew us to adoption in the first place.

When we actually did visit the orphanages, our response was somewhat different from what we expected. To us, our daughter stood out from all the other children we met. While we certainly hoped that every child would find a family, we really didn't wish that we could make them all a part of ours. Perhaps because we already had children at home, finding "the one" wasn't too difficult.

Adopting more than one child was a concept not even close to being on our radar screen. Stopping over in Germany on our first trip, however, we met a couple who told us quite matter-of-factly that they were on

their way to pick up the three children they had decided to adopt. Two of them were biological siblings; all
three were younger than the ten-year-old son who was
traveling with them.

Like us, they were adopting for the first time. They
happily enumerated the positive and challenging quali-
ties they had seen in each of the three children. This
family anticipated a rather rocky beginning in some
respects, but they were committed to making it work.
Because it was off-season for their seasonal business,
both parents planned to spend the first six months at
home to help everyone adjust to their new life together.
They were amazed by our plan to add an eighth child to
our family. But compared to what they were undertaking, our little venture seemed like nothing. While we
were all quite polite, I think each family thought the
other was more than a little crazy.

Many parents of both large and small families
choose to adopt more than one child at a time. Often,
bringing home a few children at once is the result of
trying to keep a group of biological siblings together.
In those instances, the process of adoption involves not
just welcoming individual children, but a whole set of
ready-made family relationships. The gifts of this kind
of adoption are rich. Parents who seek children find
them. Children who need parents receive them. And
brothers and sisters, who may have been lost to one
another, are secured together in one family.

There are plenty of other reasons for families to multiply rather than add when pursuing an adoption. Parents whose long-term plan includes more than one adopted child may find it easier to expand rather than repeat the process. While this may somewhat divide parental attention among the brood, children often bond to each other more quickly when they experience together the adjustments they must make. Whether a family adopts biological siblings or not, those who bring home more than one child at a time minimize both time and expense. This is especially true for those who adopt internationally.

Families who are considering adopting more than one child at a time should do their best to understand and assess the demands of parenting. That may be more difficult for couples who have not yet had children. Parents familiar with child-raising, however, should not consider themselves exempt from discernment. Each child has unique needs, and no one parenting technique works for all children. I was surprised to find that adopting our daughter required me to gain a whole new set of mommy tools (some of them power tools!).

Adopting a few children at one time may feel like creating an "instant family." But the single most important thing for any adoptive family to keep in mind is that the family they hope to build will take time. In reality, there is nothing instant about it. Being gentle with one another—and with ourselves—is essential to creating a happy and complete life together. Patience leads us to develop the generous and hospitable spirit that turns a house into a home, and a collection of individuals into a loving family.

Being created in the divine image, our lives are meant to be heavily laden with luscious and plentiful fruit. Even in the very beginning, God speaks of multiplying, not simply adding. The intention of the Father is very clear: we are to be fruitful and numerous, a "company of peoples." Almost every ancient blessing regarding family life contains a prayer for unparalleled fruitfulness.

Our God is one of abundance matched by magnificent generosity. Our heavenly Father is unwearied in his desire to give. At times we can barely comprehend all that flows from the Creator's heart. Most of us find it frightening to allow ourselves to become vulnerable to a God who wants to give us so much. We may not want to feel indebted or obligated. Similarly, we may be afraid of being overwhelmed by such a torrent of gifts. Whatever our rationale, the result is that very few of us ever accept all that God longs to give.

This reticence to receive can be very clearly seen in modern family life. Many of today's families are carefully planned, so much so that some are practically made to order. Complete openness to the gift of life through marriage is not the cultural norm. Sadly, many couples exercise a level of reproductive control that keeps them from fully accepting the generosity of a loving Father.

While there are certainly reasons to space children within a family, the challenge of love is to embrace each child that God would send us. This openness to the creative will of the Holy Spirit is no less a part of adoption than it is of childbirth. Because adoption doesn't just "happen," it is a bit easier for us to sidestep the matter. The heavenly Father's plans, however, have rarely been foiled by simple biology. Just think of Sara, Rachel, Hannah, Elizabeth, and the Blessed Virgin Mary!

If you are contemplating adopting more than one child, you have opened your heart to the inspiration of the Holy Spirit. If you can resist the impulse to plan it all out in advance, you are well on your way to becoming a disciple who knows how to follow the Spirit and how to wait for him. God blesses the cheerful giver because God himself is the most cheerful of givers. We learn to give fully, however, by first learning to graciously receive.

When the Lord sees the conditions in which we live, the unmet needs we have, and our hunger for love, God does indeed want to take all of us home. The heavenly Father hopes to adopt every single one of us. God sends us as eloquent signs of his own presence. He does so to announce the desire of his heart: to make of us a mighty and numerous people, a chosen nation, and members of the Father's family dwelling together in the household of heaven.

Holy Spirit, Spirit of Abundance, open our hearts wide enough to receive all that you long to give us. Fill our homes with life and love. Help us to welcome all the children you have planned for us. Touch us with your compassion, and give us the grace to respond with compassion to others. Make our lives fruitful and generous. Enable us to allow ourselves to become vulnerable to your inspirations. Teach us to build our family patiently. Help us to be gentle with others and with ourselves. Give us a spirit of hospitality. Guide us in adding new members to our family. Give hope to the children you will ask us to receive, and help them to receive us into their lives as well. Amen.

19

Virtual Miscarriage
Lost Referrals

> Can a woman forget her nursing child, or show no compassion for the child of her womb? Even these may forget, yet I will not forget you. See, I have inscribed you on the palms of my hands.
>
> — Isaiah 49:15–16

*E*arly in our adoption process, we were informed that Russian law gave preference to Russian families, and that foreigners were viewed as a last resort for children who needed homes. On our final day in Voronezh, Oleg, our adoption facilitator, cautioned that, until our adoption was finalized, we could lose Masha if a Russian family expressed interest in adopting her. Oleg asked how quickly we could return to Russia for a court date. He advised that moving full steam ahead through the process would reduce the possibility of losing our daughter. We decided to shoot for a court date only three weeks later.

We hadn't even left Russia and were already setting up the logistics for our return. That meant we'd be traveling again when we had just managed to recover from the last remnants of jet lag. As we parted, Oleg handed us a few additional forms (yes, more paperwork!) that we would need to complete in the short time at home. These identified Masha as the child we were going to adopt. It was wonderful to see her name next to ours instead of a blank line.

We left Russia a few days later with a great deal of excitement and a few clouds of apprehension. I remember thinking on the plane home how horrifying it would be to lose our little girl. Even though Masha was not yet legally ours, in our minds and hearts she belonged to us. We found it hard to imagine taking a different child home as our daughter. Any other child would seem like an impostor. I wondered if I could even continue with an adoption if Masha wouldn't be the smiling face waiting at the end of it all. This after having met her only a few days before and spending a grand total of about six hours together!

Adopting parents do occasionally lose a child they intend to adopt to a birth mother, the child's relatives, or even another adoptive family. The grief of losing an adoption referral can feel a lot like suffering a miscarriage—even when the best interests of the child are assured. It is common for parents dealing with a lost referral to feel angry and untrusting. Suddenly, and perhaps for reasons that may be difficult to accept, joyful expectation gives way to disappointment.

The pain of such a loss is very real. For couples that have struggled with infertility, the pain may be intensified by its familiarity. Well-intentioned friends and family may expect everyone to take it all in stride, but prospective parents who lose a referral will need time to heal. Moving on with hope is both desirable and possible. Families should go gently, however, giving themselves adequate time to grieve before reentering the process. Parents who have lost a referral observe that, even after successfully adopting another child, they remain emotionally attached to the child they "lost."

There is a mysterious force that draws us to certain children. Sometimes it operates through a photograph, or a story, or a name. Although we didn't feel an inner pull to take home every child we met, there was indeed another child who captured my heart. It was Olga, one of the little girls who had walked into the room with our daughter when we first met her. Olga, even smaller than Masha, was frail and cautious with strangers. The entire time she was in the room with us, she sat on the lap of one of the orphanage caregivers. Olya, as she was called, was a sweet child. She was obviously delighted by the little barrettes the orphanage workers had placed in her pale blonde curls. Even though I knew she was not meant for us, I prayed that Olya would find a family and that God would bless her with a new life of hope. For months after I got home, I thought about Olya. From time to time, I still do.

Miraculously, God is drawn to every one of us. The magnetic force of divine love pulls the heavenly Father's attention earthward, so much so that the Son of God came to walk with us. God finds no one somehow less desirable or attractive. The Lord lays claims to us all, committing himself fully to each one of us. Even more, God's Holy Spirit, always ready to receive us, prepares each of us to receive the fullness of divine presence.

In the midst of the uncertainties we face, it is comforting to know that a family seeking to adopt will eventually bring a child home. The path toward adoption has its share of twists and turns—some more painful than others. The challenge throughout is one of trust. Many prospective parents experience moments when it is hard to keep believing in their adoption dream. Those times, however, provide a opportunity for us to place our trust where it truly belongs: in the Holy Spirit who inspired us to adopt in the first place. Parents who do so will discover that the Spirit God sends to inspire also guides and comforts us. That very same Holy Spirit consoles and heals us when things don't go the way we expect or hope.

Though the world is full of people, God does not forget any of us. Not one is lost to the eternal heart of

God. We are etched into the palm of the Father's hand by love, whether returned or unrequited. There, we are held forever.

Ultimately, the pain of remembering our loss is far sweeter than the comfort we may find in forgetfulness. Faith teaches us that no human encounter is wasted. Every time we meet another person, we meet the One who created us all. Perhaps the child you thought was yours was meant to be someone else's all along. But the love you found in that little face, the joy you felt at the sound of that name, the plans and hopes and dreams you grasped for a time were given to you for a lasting purpose. We may never know why things unfold the way they do, but through faith we can know the One who does the unfolding. We can learn to savor all God's gifts, those that bloom for a single season as well as the perennials that frame our lives. We do so trusting that what may be lost to us cannot be lost to God.

Holy Spirit, Spirit of Solace and Consolation, we thank you for your gifts, even if they are only for a time. Give us the grace to surrender every aspect of our lives to your perfect will. Help us to accept losses without anger or despair. Show us how to grieve in your presence. Nurture hope in our hearts and faith-filled trust in our souls. Teach us

to remember with sweetness those children who were almost ours. Keep us from losing the gift of love they brought into our lives. Enable us to release them to the love of others. We ask you to give them the families they need and deserve. Remember them, as we do, and bless them. Amen.

20

Medical Mysteries
Fear of the Unknown

But just when (Joseph) had resolved to do this, an angel of the Lord appeared to him in a dream and said, "Joseph, son of David, do not be afraid to take Mary as your wife, for the child conceived in her is from the Holy Spirit. She will bear a son, and you are to name him Jesus, for he will save his people from their sins." All this took place to fulfill what had been spoken by the Lord through the prophet: "Look, the virgin shall conceive and bear a son, and they shall call him Emmanuel," which means "God is with us." When Joseph awoke from sleep, he did as the angel of the Lord commanded him; he took her as his wife....

— Matthew 1:20–24

*O*rphanage directors gave us sketchy medical histories of each of the children we met. While the process of meeting the children was not dehumanizing in any way, the whole thing felt strained and uncomfortable. Children were brought into the room a few at a time. We were expected to arrive at a choice by a process of elimination based on what we saw, felt, and heard about them. If we found a child who interested us, more detailed information would be given. If none of the children met with our approval, they would be led out of the room and a few more would parade in. Thankfully, we never got past the first group of little girls. I'm not sure I would have been able to proceed much further. The only thing that seemed to make the experience fair was the fact that the Russian Ministry of Education had been given our medical and personal histories as well. I guess, in that respect, it was an even trade.

As soon as we expressed interest in the possibility of adopting Masha, we were led into the director's office. We listened as Masha's medical files were read out loud and then translated into English. Because her entry into the world had not been officially recorded until her orphanage placement, very little was known about Masha's birth. Her birth mother's name did not appear on the government registry of alcoholics or drug addicts. Nonetheless, after the State took custody of her, Masha spent some time in the hospital for medical evaluation. She was diagnosed—as almost every Russian orphan is—with "resid-

ual perinatal encephalopathy." This shocking terminology, we later learned, denoted a condition entirely
unfamiliar to American doctors, and is applied with
little or no substantiation. Her Russian lab tests for
HIV, hepatitis, and other communicable diseases were
all clear.

Masha sat up at about ten months, and did not
walk until she was fifteen months old. She was alleg-
edly toilet-trained (more accurately, toilet-timed). At
thirty-four months, Masha was just beginning to talk
(in Russian, of course!). She didn't catch cold often,
but the files noted a "breath-holding incident"—whatever that was. She had fallen down once and been hos-
pitalized with stitches on her forehead. Nothing was
said about how very small Masha was, except that she
weighed ten kilos, and was only eighty centimeters
tall. My math-friendly husband quickly did the calcu-
lations and got twenty-two pounds and thirty-one
inches, the size of an average American child at about
fifteen months. All of the children in the orphanage
were tiny and underdeveloped; Masha was not unique
in that respect.

There was something very unsettling about hearing what was contained in those files. I felt as if the
information we were being given was, in some sense,
none of our business. The folder held everything that
could be told about Masha, but it didn't take long
to read. What struck me most was how much more

information I had tucked into my brain about our other children's early years. I knew what they weighed at birth. I remembered when they slept through the night, what foods they loved, and the baby talk they used to my delight (like "te-low-low" for telephone, and "yakoo guk" for chocolate milk). I had photographs of our babies reaching and rolling, sitting and standing and walking. What I knew about their first three years would fill a book much longer than this one. It became clear that whatever the orphanage director could tell us about Masha's health and medical history would be just a few pieces of a vastly larger puzzle.

Because of our family's limitations, medical issues were a key part of our discernment process. With responsibility for so many kids, we had already decided that it was best to avoid a child with ongoing health problems if at all possible. I had heard of adoptive families hiring American physicians to examine children at overseas orphanages. Other medical professionals at home specialized in reviewing videos of children available for adoption, as well as their medical records. Feeling a level of confidence we hadn't expected, we decided not to avail ourselves of those options.

Instead, interacting with Masha, we chose to trust our instincts and rather extensive hands-on pediatric experience. Having a two-and-a-half-year-old at home gave us a pretty good developmental yardstick to go by, and Masha did not seem very far behind. If there were medical issues, we were confident in our ability to handle them. Later, the doctor who examined Masha in Moscow generally confirmed our assessment. He agreed that aside from a mild case of rickets due to poor nutrition, Masha's health appeared to be what her records indicated. We were more than satisfied.

Not long after we brought her home, however, Masha was bitten by a dog. As hospital workers began to ask questions regarding her medical history, we realized how few answers we really had. Everything seemed fine until an emergency room nurse gave Masha intravenous penicillin. It took less than five minutes to discover that she was allergic to it. Her whole body broke out in a rash. The emergency room nurse pulled the IV immediately, and a doctor prescribed a completely different oral antibiotic to take home. Before we left, we were told that the medication Masha was given was not nearly as effective as penicillin. Later that night, she spiked a high fever that led to a febrile seizure. Completely alarmed by what was happening, my mind immediately went back to the mysterious "breath-holding" mentioned in Masha's file. Suddenly, we worried about what else might come up. We felt as though we had been walking blithely through a minefield without even knowing it.

Eventually, the doctors discovered that the dog bite had been compounded by a urinary tract infection that

Masha had probably had when we took custody of her in Russia. Things ran their course, however, and settled down. As the time of crisis passed, we realized that our fears had been magnified by the stress of the situation. Masha has never had another seizure since, and all her medical files now note her allergy to penicillin.

Fear about a child's medical history can cripple parents seeking to adopt. Often, there is an impulse to confirm and reconfirm; to get as many medical opinions and reviews as possible. Serious health issues may merit that kind of attention. But when it comes to more general concerns, there really is no way to know every detail of our adoptive children's health or medical history. No matter how diligent we are in seeking information, some relevant facts are bound to be left out.

Those unknowns, however, are also present for families with biological children. Realizing that I could have given birth to a child with medical problems made me much more willing to accept what I did not know about Masha. Any one of our other kids could suddenly come down with a serious illness, or be diagnosed with a medical condition that I would not have knowingly accepted if I had the choice.

It was also helpful to understand that health is more of a continuum than a standard. Discussing our plan to adopt with our pediatrician, I had asked how best to avoid a child with fetal alcohol syndrome

(FAS) or effects (FAE). He advised me not to be over-
ly concerned about accepting a child who was at risk
for either one. The range of symptoms, he said, was
so huge that it would be practically impossible to
know how much a child would be affected by such a
condition. Many children had so few problems that
there was no compelling reason to ever seek a diagnosis.

Love means committing to each other for better or
for worse. Usually, we get a portion of both. In that
respect, raising children is a lot like getting married.
Both biological and adoptive families take risks with
and for each other. There are no guarantees for the
children we bring home from a hospital nursery, or for
those we bring home from a courtroom. Whether or
not we fully know a child's past, we cannot know what
the future holds or how that individual child will welcome it.

Fear is a natural response to uncertainty. Even
Joseph was afraid to fully commit himself to Mary and
her child. That is why, in the midst of his restless
nights, the Lord sent an angel to reassure Joseph with
a dream. Telling him that Mary's child was conceived
by the power of the Holy Spirit, the angel called Joseph
from fear to faith. Love always brings forth trust in the
face of anxiety. Joseph took Mary into his house
because he was convinced that this was God's plan not
only for her, but also for himself.

It is wonderful to realize that the Holy Family was both biological and adoptive. Mary gave birth to Jesus, and Joseph adopted him. Neither one of them fully understood what would be required of them as parents of the Son of God, nor could they comprehend the depth of God's gift to us all in Christ. If medical mysteries stir up worry in your heart, just wait for the "angel" God sends in the people we love and trust. God will always give us the assurance we need to live out his divine will for us. The Holy Spirit will lead you through fear into faith. In doing so, God will establish in your heart love that cannot fail.

Holy Spirit, Divine Healer, give health to us and to our children. As we follow your plan, help us to understand all the medical information we receive. Teach us to give more weight to a person than to a diagnosis. Give us the grace to know our limitations and the prudence to live within them. Guard us from fear and free us from anxiety. Encourage us in love. Strengthen our resolve to choose love, especially in the face of what is unknown to us. Enable us to trust you when there are risks. Lead us from fear into faith. Send us all the reassurance we need. Keep us, and the children you are keeping for us, in the shelter of your embrace. Amen.

21

The Burden of History
Why Your Child Is Available

> As for your birth, on the day you were born
> your navel cord was not cut, nor were you
> washed with water to cleanse you, nor
> rubbed with salt, nor wrapped with cloths. No
> eye pitied you, to do any of these things for
> you out of compassion for you; but you were
> thrown out in the open field, for you were
> abhorred on the day you were born. I passed
> by you, and saw you flailing about in your
> blood. As you lay in your blood, I said to you,
> "Live! and grow up like a plant of the field."
> — Ezekiel 16:4–6

When we first met Masha she walked into the room with attitude. She was an obvious limelighter, adept at getting the attention every orphanage child needed, but few ever got. Her techniques were both

subtle and endearing. They were certainly effective on us! When we heard about Masha's background, we knew why she had become so good at working a crowd. It was her way of exercising some control over her life. The orphanage director and our adoption facilitator summarized what they called Masha's "social history." Neither of us was really sure what a "social history" was or how a two-year-old could have one. As they began to talk, however, we found out.

Masha's birth was never reported or officially recorded. She didn't even have a birth certificate until she was placed in the orphanage at nine months. When she got one, the space next to the word "father" was left blank. Her birth mother had never been married. She lived with a series of boyfriends in a boarding house. Masha was not her first child, neither was she the first to be taken away by the State for reasons of neglect. We were told that when she was removed, government workers could not find any food in the house for a nine-month-old child. For whatever reason, or complex of reasons, Masha's birth mother was not living a lifestyle that was suitable for children. No elaboration was given, except that she had never called or written the orphanage to ask about Masha.

I suppose that in some ways Masha's story inspired me. She was exactly the kind of child we had hoped to find, one who desperately needed what we had to give.

While it was hard to choke back the tears, I could sense great hope for Masha's situation. Realizing that we held the power to change her life was as humbling as it was exciting. All we had to do was act on the compassion that Masha's story had enkindled in us.

The injustice this poor child suffered made us indignant at some level. But the little girl we saw dancing and twirling before us was not angry, although she had every right to be. She was as charming as any child—even as engaging as the ones we had left at home. Hearing Masha's history was very sad indeed. At not even three years old, she had experienced far more than her share of grief. No child deserves that kind of life.

There was a tangible reticence among the orphanage staff in telling us about Masha's past. It was almost as if they expected us to cross Masha's name off our list. Most of Masha's portrait was blank canvas. There were next to no details, and those that were known were all negatives. Masha's needs—even her most basic needs—had not been met. Orphanage life had been a step up from where she had been before. The picture the staff painted was not a pretty one, and they knew it. Yet the child standing in front of us, the little girl holding a hand as she walked around the room, was very pretty indeed. Despite the negative things we heard, in that moment it was clear to us that Masha's past did not have to dictate her future. Where she came from did not have the power to determine where she was going...because she was going with us.

It is important for prospective parents to remember that the reasons they are able to adopt a child are often very sad. Our children come to us from death, poverty, addiction, racism, sexism, abuse, neglect, irresponsibility, social policies, and even war. While most of us have not lived with any of those horrors, many of our adoptive children have. The wounds they bear present us with opportunities to practice sensitivity and to learn the art of healing love. Adoption is the sweet fruit that miraculously falls from bitter trees.

Our God knows every burden we bear and all the sacrifices that have been made by us and for us. The Holy One knew the pain Joshebed felt when she placed her infant son afloat in a basket on the Nile. The Lord saw Mordecai's willingness to raise his young orphaned cousin Hadassah as his own daughter. The Almighty looks at each of us with compassion and stoops to care for us when no one else will. God sees our dilemmas and reaches toward us with love that leads.

Divine love leads us all. Love led Pharaoh's daughter to take an abandoned Hebrew boy as her son. Love led the King of Persia to choose Hadassah—that is, Esther—as his wife. And even more, love led Moses, a Prince of Egypt, to deliver his people from slavery, and Esther to defend her people as their Queen. Both

Moses and Esther were adopted children. Their origins were simply that, the place their lives began.

None of us ends where we begin. Each of us carries the burden of a personal history, but what we carry does not have to set our direction or our course. The issues adoptive children face as they grow up depend on what is woven into their own personal stories. Some threads of color may be painful to hear or remember. The truth in all its fullness can be received if it is told in love. The gift of family, however, enables something even more wonderful. For when the truth is shared in love, the beauty of the fabric as a whole can be seen and embraced.

Holy Spirit, Father of the Poor, inspire in us compassion for the weak. Show us your power to bring good from evil, joy from sorrow, healing and wholeness from pain. Keep us mindful of all who are in need, especially those to whom you have called us. Give us grace not to judge others by their personal histories. Help us not to be ashamed of them or for them. Teach us that the past does not have to dictate the future. Empower us to change that little piece of the world in which we live. Enable us, too, to be changed by those we meet. In sharing the truth, give us a glimpse of your hand at work in our children's lives. Weave us together as one family sharing an eternity that is yet to come. Amen.

22

Are You My Mother?
Birth and Adoptive Mothers

Then the king said, "The one says, 'This is my son that is alive, and your son is dead'; while the other says, 'Not so! Your son is dead, and my son is the living one.'" So the king said, "Bring me a sword," and they brought a sword before the king. The king said, "Divide the living boy in two; then give half to the one and half to the other."

— 1 Kings 3:23–25

*I*t was difficult to listen to the orphanage workers explain the neglect that Masha had suffered. As a mother, I could not imagine allowing a child to be neglected as Masha had been. I only wished that I had been there to prevent it all from happening. The whole thing made me angry.

While righteous indignation may have a place, mine was perhaps not so righteous. Struggling to keep myself from feeling intrinsically superior to Masha's birth mother, Irina, I found it downright impossible to resist the temptation to blame her. The problem was that I had just enough information to know how Masha had been treated, but not nearly enough information to understand why. In the midst of that knowledge gap, I found it very easy to despise the woman who gave her birth. In my mind, she was not entitled to claim motherhood of any kind.

Still, there were pieces of Masha's story that didn't fit, aspects of the story that didn't make much sense to me at the time. Abortion is very common throughout Russia, and has been for many years. If a woman didn't want a child, there was a socially acceptable—if not morally acceptable—way out. If, thank God, she opposed abortion, other options were available to her. Orphanages in Russia aren't just for orphans. They aren't even called "orphanages," but "baby houses" and "children's homes." Any woman could relinquish her maternal rights and place her child in a nearby facility. A struggling mother could arrange a temporary placement and would be able to maintain contact with her child. If her situation improved, she could reclaim custody. If not, she could decide to release the child for possible adoption. Masha's birth mother didn't do any of these things. Instead, she hid her daughter's birth from the authorities. She had lost one child to them before.

The real puzzle wasn't fitting the pieces of Masha's past together, but trying to understand how I could, in the same moment, have so much compassion for a child and hold so much contempt for the woman who gave her life. I realized that in order to overcome my profoundly negative feelings toward Masha's birth mother, I would have to move way beyond the facts. Instead of envisioning what I knew about her background, I began to create scenarios about what I didn't know. Grasping for understanding, I used my imagination to fill in the gaps. By concocting countless scenes and vignettes, and by thinking of her by name, Masha's birth mother became more human to me. Trying to get inside Irina's mind, I could begin to allow her a place in my heart.

While I may never be able to develop a purely positive opinion of Irina, I can continue to cultivate a willingness to understand her plight. However distorted or inadequate her love, Irina loved her daughter. The truth is that while I have mixed feelings about her, most likely so does Masha. Even more, I wonder how Irina felt when she was notified that a foreign family had adopted her daughter. It is very possible that she had, at best, mixed feelings toward us.

While it can be difficult for an adoptive family to accept, a child's birth parents are always part of his or her life. That is true whether or not they share an ongoing relationship, and whether or not the relationship has been positive or negative for the child. Doing what we can to keep a charitable view of an adopted child's family of origin affirms the child's whole identity. The story of the two mothers in the court of Solomon can teach us something about the struggle between birth and adoptive parents. Two women approach the king claiming to be the child's mother. Knowing that they cannot both be right, Solomon orders the infant to be cut in two and divided between them. The child's true mother is the one who is willing to give him up in order to save his life.

I believe that a drama very much like this is played out in the mind of the adoptive child. Wondering who her mother really is, she imagines a dispute between the two women who claim her. Believing that only one woman can be her mother, the solution she constructs to the dilemma she faces demands that she is torn in two. The struggle between mothers within the child can leave her identity fragmented and her loyalties divided.

The adoptive family must take up the challenge to think more creatively and flexibly. Parents who adopt do not need to "give up" their child in order to prove the validity of their claim. What they can do, however, is to think kindly of their children's birth parents, and teach them to do the same. The result will be a whole

child with two mothers, rather than two childless
women.

Children need a mother to give them life, and a
mother to give them love. These gifts are not necessarily given to a child by the same woman. Adoption is
based on recognizing that possibility. Still, both women
have a critical role to play. Both are the child's "real"
mother.

Jesus asked the same question many adoptive families find themselves wondering. "Who is my mother,
and who are my brothers and sisters?" (Mt 12:48–50)
The answer he gave was not as obvious as one might
expect. The mother of Jesus is the one who hears the
word of God and does it. (Probably the best description
of Mary ever!) Those who do the will of the Father are
brothers and sisters to the Son of God. What Jesus was
telling us is something that in all likelihood we already
knew. Our eternal family is made up of the people who
love and care for one another. Blood may be thicker
than water, but love trumps them both!

If the feelings you have toward your child's birth
family are confused or conflicted, you have gained a
window into the emotional life of your child. We need
not feel threatened by the fact that our children were
not born to us. Life and love are meant to go together.
All who love give life. Those who give life, in some
measure, also love.

Holy Spirit, Spirit of Meekness and Humility, give us hearts that know and accept the truth about ourselves, and eyes that see others the way you see them. Teach us how to forgive those who have hurt the children you have called us to love. Help us to be grateful for those who gave them life and bless them. Fill us with a willingness to understand the pain they may have suffered, too. Keep us from competing with them or considering ourselves superior to them in any way. Teach our children kindness and forgiveness through us. Transform all our lives by the power of your love. Amen.

23
What's in a Name?
Identity: Who and Whose

The daughter of Pharaoh came down to bathe at the river, while her attendants walked beside the river. She saw the basket among the reeds and sent her maid to bring it. When she opened it, she saw the child. He was crying, and she took pity on him. "This must be one of the Hebrews' children," she said. ...When the child grew up, (the woman) brought him to Pharaoh's daughter, and she took him as her son. She named him Moses, "because," she said, "I drew him out of the water."

— Exodus 2:5–10

*A*s soon as our homestudy was underway, there was great interest and discussion in our house about what name we were going to give to the newest kid on

161

the block. Everyone got into the act, and everyone had an opinion. One thing was non-negotiable: the name had to be Russian. Of course, that presented little difficulty, as most of our children had Slavic names anyway. It wasn't easy to picture a Russian child looking like a Madison or a Jennifer.

Planning to bring home a baby, we figured that the choice was pretty much ours. It didn't take long for Anastasia to rise to the top of the list. I was convinced that Anastasia was the perfect name. It sounded good, produced several possible nicknames, and belonged to one of the last Russian princesses. Best of all, it meant "resurrection." Anastasia, in fact, had been a hardy perennial on our list of baby names. It had been edged out by the narrowest of margins on our last trip into the delivery room.

When we actually traveled to Russia, the rules of our name game changed rather abruptly. Deciding to adopt a toddler rather than an infant meant that our daughter already had a name—one that she used for herself and answered to. We couldn't imagine asking Masha to answer to anything else. Her name was already too much a part of her emerging identity.

Suddenly, we had a bit of a problem. "Masha" is not often or easily heard by the American ear. On the other hand, her full name—Maria—was more common in the United States than any of the names we had given our other children. It just didn't fit with the rest of the family. We decided that our best approach would be to extend Maria to Marianna. In that way, Masha could have a new name—one that we had given her—without losing the name she already had. Because Anna means "grace," we figured that what we were doing was adding grace to Maria. We continued to call her Masha and Maria, but that extra syllable was there for her when and if she ever wanted it.

Names are important. If they weren't, we wouldn't have entire bookstore shelves filled with volumes offering advice and lists for naming your baby. And though I have never looked, I'm convinced that there must also be books out there written to help name your dog, cat, or goldfish too. ("Do you think 'Fluffy' is just too old-fashioned?") Parents—both birth and adoptive—give the matter of naming a child a great deal of attention. We do so because we know that names express identity. They reveal something about who we are, and whose we are as well. Even more, our names influence how we see ourselves.

Naming presents a unique set of considerations for families who adopt. Unless they are adopting a newborn, parents come to realize that giving an adopted child a name usually means changing one he already has. Prospective parents may choose a name for their child even before receiving a referral. For them, accepting a child for adoption means that they have found Jacob or Molly. Many, however, wait until they meet their new son or daughter, and then try to find a balance between their own desires and what a child already brings with him or her.

There is a wide range of opinion about how much deference parents ought to give to the name a child possessed before adoption. When the surname is going to change regardless, the importance of maintaining the connection to what a child has been called is open to debate. Some parents keep an original first name as a middle name. Others translate the child's name into an English equivalent. Still others give their children names that include connections to birth and/or adoptive relations. While at times it may seem as if a child's name has been decided by committee, beautiful and creative ideas abound.

Names, both old and new, express not only family ties, but also cultural connections. While maintaining a child's culture is a worthy pursuit, many adoptive families are careful to avoid any difficulties their children may have with their peers. Parents may decide to change a particularly unusual name, for example, to something less obtrusive. For me, Ivan would have been fine, but Igor? I don't think so.

Choosing to keep your child's name or trade it in for a new one is ultimately a matter of personal preference. The truth is that both old and new names can hold rich significance for a child. Parents may be less willing to name change if they know that it is their child's only possession, the only thing he really owns. Old names, too, can provide a sense of continuity for a child, and security in his own identity. A new name, on the other hand, can help a child reinforce his belonging to a new family. For children coming from difficult backgrounds, a new name may reassure them that they are being given a whole new life.

Among the great heroes of the Bible, few names resound as powerfully as Moses. Yet, if we stop to think about it, we realize that Moses was the name given to Israel's deliverer by the daughter of Pharaoh. It was an Egyptian rather than a Hebrew name, given by the child's adoptive mother and not his birth mother. We will never know what Joshebed called him as she wrapped him in a blanket and set him afloat on the river. No name other than Moses is ever mentioned.

Throughout the Bible, God gives new names to people when the divine Initiator is doing something new. Abram and Sarai became Abraham and Sarah. Jacob became Israel. Simon was called Peter, and Saul became Paul. As Christians, we keep this tradition when we are given new names at Confirmation or at religious profession. These names express the new mission our Father envisions for us and are meant to inspire us to attain the holiness of those who answered to them before.

The prophet Isaiah tells us, "The nations shall see your vindication and all the kings your glory, and you shall be called by a new name that the mouth of the Lord will give" (Is 62:2). Ultimately, God promises each of us a new name. While they are mysterious and unknown to us, they are kept in the mouth of our heavenly Father. What we know, however, is this: the names God gives us will reflect not only who we are, but also who we were made to become. We will be called by a name that announces we belong to the God of heaven. That glory will be the vindication of us all. And more, it will be our joy!

Holy Spirit, Breath of God, you call us each by name. Give us the grace to know who we are, and to be fully who you created us to be. Help us to recognize your voice. Seal us as your own. Inspire us to give our children names they can embrace with all their hearts. Enable them to begin anew with the knowledge that they belong not only to us, but to you. Strengthen in them their identity as children beloved by the Father. Give them the certainty of our acceptance. Protect them from isolation. Build in them a strong sense of self. Help them to be proud not only of what they are called, but of whom they are called to be. Amen.

24
The Waiting Child
Your Child's Daily Life

But you do see! Indeed you note trouble and
grief, that you may take it into your hands;
the helpless commit themselves to you; you
have been the helper of the orphan.
— Psalm 10:14

Three days after we met Masha, we returned
to the orphanage to confirm our desire to adopt her.
We were quickly ushered into the director's office.
Alla sat across the desk wearing a very serious face.
She asked us again, through the translator, if we real-
ly wanted Masha. We told her that while it had taken
a few days to communicate with the rest of our fami-
ly at home, we knew that Masha was meant for us.
As the translator spoke our words into Russian,
Alla smiled broadly. She was so happy to see Masha

find a family that she was almost giddy. Then she told us why.

Alla also had hoped to adopt a little girl. Knowing that she had been thinking about finding a daughter, the hospital had called her when Masha was brought in. Instead of sending Masha to another nearby baby house, they sent her to Alla. Alla loved Masha very much—she doted on her, as much as any child could be doted on in an institutional setting. At some point, however, she realized that adopting a child, any child, would be too much for her. For Masha's sake, Alla decided to actively seek another adoptive family for her.

After we signed the orphanage book pledging ourselves to Masha, Alla took us upstairs to tell her that we would be her mama and papa. She told Masha that she would have to listen to us, do what she was told, be a good girl, and keep herself clean. Alla explained that she would have a family now, and that we would soon come back to take her home. We gave Masha the musical toy we had brought with us, as well as the "Who Loves Baby" photo album with pictures of our whole family inside. As Masha threw her arms around us, Alla left the room. I sensed that even though there were 120 children living there, Masha would be missed terribly—at least by Alla.

It was clear to us that our daughter had been loved. The director and caregivers all gave something to Masha. While none of them could give her all that she needed, they had done what they could. Some had even opened their hearts. We felt sad to leave Russia without Masha, especially because we really didn't know how long it would take to get a court date. Yet, we knew that she would be cared for in our absence, and that every attempt would be made to prepare her for her new life with us.

Few of us will ever fully appreciate what it is like living day to day in an orphanage, or in foster care, or to be without family relationships. Our daughter's life was completely regimented. There were no choices for her to make; no questions for her to answer. She ate, slept, and went to the bathroom by the clock. She slept in just her underwear, and wore the same dress for a week. Her shoes didn't quite fit, but she loved them because they were turquoise with little butterflies. She played with toys that weren't hers. Nothing, in fact, was. While she buzzed with delight about going "home," she really didn't know what a home was. Neither did she know the difference between an orphanage caregiver and a mother or father.

Many children awaiting adoption are not exactly sure what it is they are waiting for. Still, I think children understand that there is no substitute for a family that loves them. Even if family life is completely foreign to them, even if past experiences of family relationships hurt them, kids know what they need. While we could hardly wait to take Masha home with us, she passed the time with even greater anxiety and anticipation. Thankfully, her wait wasn't long. Exactly one week and two days after returning from Russia, we received a court date.

We returned to Russia only three weeks after we had left. Knowing that three weeks is an eternity to a child, we weren't sure how Masha would respond to us. But, catching a glimpse of Andrew and me through a window, she burst through the door laughing so hard she could barely breathe. She was so excited she couldn't contain herself; that night, we made sure that we learned the Russian word for "calm"—*spacoina!*

Alla also told us that, during the three weeks before our return to Voronezh, Masha had stopped eating and would not let go of the toy and photo album we had given her. But the most amazing thing was how much Masha's language had improved in just three weeks. Alla told us that she had seen this happen before. Children who knew that they were going home often had a burst of development, especially in language. Talking had become more important to Masha because now she had someone she wanted to talk to.

We returned to the orphanage to see Masha as soon as we had completed our court proceedings on the following day, stopping only to purchase a new computer for the orphanage out of money donated by well-wishers back in the United States. Masha was more than ready to go home; she expected that we would be able to take her with us immediately. Unfortunately, that was not the case. There were several bureaucratic stops that we would have to make the next morning. In a flurry of activity, we needed to obtain Masha's Russian passport, adoption certificate, and a new birth certificate that named us as Masha's parents. (It made it seem as if I had given birth to her while traveling in Russia!) When we told her that we would have to come back for her the next day, Masha exploded into uncontrollable tears.

Holding her close, I repeated the Russian word for "tomorrow." *"Zaftra...zaftra...."* After a few minutes she joined the mantra and calmed down. Reminding her she still had her photo book of family pictures seemed to help, too. As we left, I was the one who broke down. Obviously, the waiting had been much harder on her than it could ever have been on us.

Many adults have struggled through years hoping to have a baby. Adoptive parents pass months in anticipation of bringing a child home. But however long it takes for us, our children have waited their entire lives to experience what it means to have a home. Every moment of their days has been spent wishing, perhaps unconsciously, for parents who are able to love them the way they need to be loved.

The Holy Spirit works to bring families and children together. God is always coming up with new ways to inspire us to do things that surprise even ourselves. The Creator leads us to adoption. The Paraclete encourages us to wade through mountains of paperwork. The Spirit convinces some of us to embrace strangers as members of our families. Others of us find ourselves hopping onto airplanes destined for places we've never even heard of!

Still, that is only half the story. For the very same Holy Spirit that guides you is also with your children before you meet them, before you even know them to be yours. God sees their need and takes it into his loving hands. Our heavenly Father is the helper of orphans. We can trust that even when we must leave them behind, they will be kept alive by the Spirit of God. Looking forward with faith to the day of our children's homecoming, we can begin to understand that we merely share in what God has been doing all along in our absence. All our lives, God loves, cares, calls, and waits for each of us to come home to him.

Holy Spirit, Spiritual Balm, you loved our children before we knew anything about them. Before we could care for them, you kept them alive. When others could not meet all their needs, you sustained them. Help us to think well of those who did their best to provide for our children before they were ours. Bless them in the demands of their daily

work. Give them hearts of compassion for the children in their care. Help us to give our children the home they long for, the one they have waited for all their lives. When our love comes up short, fill in the gaps with the ointment of your mercy. Provide for us all from the richness of your grace. Amen.

25
Love at First Sight?
Meeting Your Child

Arise, my love, my fair one, come away...let
me see your face, let me hear your voice; for
your voice is sweet and your face is lovely.
— Song of Songs 2:13b; 14b

*M*asha had mesmerized us from the moment we saw her; we felt an instant connection to her from the start. It was a force we did not expect to encounter, certainly one far more formidable than any we had anticipated. We still can't quite figure out how such a skinny little wisp of a girl could wield such power!

Masha's personality had us wrapped around her little finger in no time flat. We felt drawn to her, attracted by everything we saw in her tiny but irresistible self. Peering deeply into our eyes when we spoke, she responded with delight to every ounce of attention we gave her. Masha was affectionate and energetic. Looking intently at the family photo album we had brought along, she attempted to learn all the names of the strangers she saw inside. She was happy to try anything we suggested, even English.

While Masha did not yet know how to count, she had no trouble doing math. She suspected right away that the two of us added up to something wonderful for her! Whatever that something was, she was game to go after it. After all was said and done, Masha's plan won out. Somehow, without words, she convinced us to abandon the idea of adopting an infant, and take her home instead.

While I was completely head-over-heels infatuated with Masha, I can't say that I loved her in those first moments, or days, or weeks. She was different from our homegrown children, but enough like them that I could see it would not be difficult to love her. The truth is that Masha was, in some ways, a novelty. This little girl speaking Russian baby talk, trapped on the other side of the world, needed us and she knew it. It felt good to be needed like that.

It was easy to love the idea of loving Masha, and we committed our lives to that idea. I remember wondering if I could ever love her as much as I did our other children. I wondered because I knew that right then and there I didn't. In time, I knew it was possible to love her that way...because I did.

Thousands of families claim to have loved their adopted children at first sight. Somehow, I think that "love" may be overstating things a bit. We can certainly perceive a personal chemistry or connection. We may also be deeply drawn to a particular child. Real love, however, both gives and takes much more than that.

It is unreasonable to expect that every photo, video, or first meeting with a child will fill every adoptive parent with a rush of spontaneous or overwhelming love. Many parents do not experience a special attraction to the child they expect to adopt. Some feel more estranged than connected. The truth is that few of us find every child equally attractive. In fact, we are bound to meet up with some children who—like some adults—turn us off. We may not even be able to pinpoint the reasons why.

First meetings may be difficult for family members who experience little or no emotion toward a child referred to them for adoption. Waiting to be hit by a romantic ton of bricks, parents may find themselves tempted to turn down a referral simply because the child does not evoke in them a strong emotional response.

Love, however, does not depend on how—or even if—we feel. Infatuation is not the stuff of parenting, commitment is. The truth is that parents fall in and out of love with their children just as they fall in and out of love with each other. There are days of sweetness and

affection, to be sure. But there are also seasons of annoyance and frustration. It is amazing how the child I was so happy to see in the morning can be the same child I am relieved to be putting to bed that night.

Ultimately, love is an act of will: a conscious and deliberate decision to devote ourselves to what is good for another. Faith is persevering in the decision to love. Because love is so much more than a feeling, it can grow despite any lack of feeling we may have. When we choose to love, we choose to grow in that love. We do not start out in full bloom. Adoption, like marriage, is a sprout from which the fragrant flowers of love may bud and blossom in time.

We can't genuinely love each other at first sight. God can, but even more, our heavenly Father manages to love us before first sight. Each of us is the result of that love. We exist simply because God loves us into being.

The Lord's love for us does not grow. It begins in fullness and is a flower that never fades. While our love for the Holy One can wax and wane, the divine love we enjoy is ever constant. The Creator knows everything about his creation. There is nothing that our Father needs to discover about us. All things are seen by heaven's eyes.

In God's eyes every one of us is "fair and lovely." Our Father's great desire is to see the faces formed by his own hands, and to hear the voices he gave us raised in song. The Holy Spirit invites each of us to arise and come. God leaves no one uninvited. The eternal wedding supper of the lamb is meant to gather all people as guests of the Most High.

Perhaps you have heard God's call in your own soul. When you decide to love, you are allowing that invitation to echo through your life. In committing yourself to loving a child, you are committing yourself to passing along the very same invitation you received. There is no better RSVP we can give to the Holy Spirit.

Holy Spirit, Consuming Fire, enkindle in us a steadfast love for the children you have given us. Help us to look beyond those things that attract or repel us. Guard us against unrealistic or romantic expectations. Show us how to love by choice as well as by emotion. Give us faith to persevere and patience that allows time and space for love to grow. Teach us to pass through days that are chill; to set aside our own need to be loved for the sake of loving our children well. Burn in our hearts as the source of the love we share. Enflame us with the warmth of your passion toward us, and help us to share that warmth with one another. Amen.

26

Your Day in Court
Lawyers, Judges, and Legalese

> "When they bring you before the synagogues, the rulers and the authorities, do not worry about how you are to defend yourselves or what you are to say; for the Holy Spirit will teach you at that very hour what you ought to say."
>
> — Luke 12:11

*O*n our second trip to Russia, we were picked up at the Moscow airport and told that we would be taking a train to Voronezh, a ten-hour journey.

The previous three weeks at home had been a blur of activity. Waiting for confirmation of our court date, we still had to complete and apostille a few additional forms. When we finally received the call with our actual court date, we had less than a week to book our flights. This time, we added a third—one way—ticket home. While I was completely exhausted from the trip across eight time zones, I found it impossible to sleep on the overnight train. The "bed" was comfortable enough, but I couldn't sleep through the noise of the tracks and the excitement of what we were about to do. Looking out the window in the middle of the night, I was struck by how many stars I could see in the Russian sky. It was as black as the earth we were traveling across, now that the winter snows had begun to melt. In the three weeks between trips, spring had come.

We arrived in Voronezh early on a Sunday morning, and spent the day visiting Masha and preparing for our appearance in a Russian court the following day. Our facilitator, Oleg, told us that the judge would probably ask a few questions, and, guessing at what they might be, Oleg listened to the answers we would give.

Arriving at the court, we were introduced to the attorney who would represent us, a young man who seemed pleased with the kind of work he was doing. Our translator, Ina, accompanied us into the courtroom, where we saw one of the orphanage caregivers and a woman we were told was an official from the region's Ministry of Education. Oleg stayed outside. That made Andrew and me even more nervous. The room itself was small and in terrible disrepair. As I wondered if anything really official could happen there,

the judge walked in. An older man sure of his authority, he came across as a bit gruff and more than a bit
intimidating. His face reminded me of the political car-
toons I had seen as a child at the height of the Cold
War. Andrew thought he looked more like an old
Boston judge appointed by some official his cousin had
helped get re-elected. We sat down, and the proceedings began.

The facts of Masha's history and her medical prognosis were read aloud. The representatives from the
government and the orphanage gave their statements
in turn. Mostly, they emphasized how dim her future
appeared, and exaggerated any developmental issues
Masha might have, in order to give the judge even
more reason to approve our adoption and waive the
usual ten-day waiting period, which could extend our
time in Russia. It took less than two minutes for our
attorney to present a summary of the mountain of
paperwork we had been required to submit—the one
that had taken months to assemble. The judge
thumbed through our dossier. Then he asked the question we had rehearsed the day before with Oleg: "Why
would anyone with seven children want to adopt another one?"

My husband stood up and talked about how much
he loved children, how they were the light of his life,
how he could not imagine living without them. The
judge seemed unimpressed. I suppose he thought that a

man's love for children should be satisfied with two or three of them, let alone seven. It didn't seem to adequately explain a desire for an eighth child. Then it was my turn. Taking a different tack, I spoke about how we viewed adoption as being about not just what we could give to a child who needs a family, but also what that child would bring to us. Adopting Masha, I said, was a way to teach our children generosity of heart, and to experience how family is made by love that crosses every boundary, even birth, language, and culture. I'm not sure the judge fully appreciated the sentiments of my speech, but he was satisfied (or perplexed) enough to move on to question number two.

The second question was a lot easier to answer. "Why did you come to Russia instead of going somewhere else?" My husband talked about my Slavic heritage. Culturally, our family had some circuitous tie to the Russian people. The fact that it probably dated back to the migration of the Slavs from the Asian steppes did not appear to deter the judge. Reading the names of our other children, "Jana, Katerina, Kyril," he asked if we had adopted the rest of our kids from Russia as well. When we told him they were all biological, he shook his head and stood up to leave the room. Twenty minutes later, the judge returned and announced that Masha was now our daughter Marianna.

Courtrooms and legal proceedings make everyone nervous. Our obligations under the law and the number of procedures we must follow are serious business. Unfortunately, judges, lawyers, and stenographers can create a level of anxiety that clouds the love that motivates us to adopt. At times, what is going on can be confusing and hard to understand. Whether the court is American or not, legalese in any place is a foreign language. We never know what we will be asked (I think Oleg predicted the first question because he has six children of his own). But whatever questions are posed, all we need to do is answer.

The Spirit that inspires also teaches us. God promises, in fact, that when we need the right words, we will find that he has placed them on our tongues. When we are brought before authorities of any kind, we need not worry about how we will acquit ourselves. The Holy Spirit will teach us what to do, and God will empower us to do or say what is necessary.

Like the judges in adoption courts, God creates families out of strangers. The letter to the Ephesians explains, "You are no longer strangers and aliens, but you are citizens with the saints, and also members of the household of God" (Eph 2:19). The child you will call your own, the one you will love for a lifetime and beyond, was once completely unknown to you. Foreigners, aliens with no connection to one another, by God's grace we all become members of one heavenly household. There is nothing for us to fear, for our judge is also our Father.

Holy Spirit, Divine Teacher, place in our mouths the words we need. Give us courage before those who will judge us. Empower us to answer what is asked of us with confidence and truth. Protect us from nervousness and confusion. Inspire in us a respect for authority and law. Bless the judge before whom we will appear, the lawyers and courtroom workers. Help them to appreciate the importance of what they do for families. Help us all to seek your will and to see your work to completion. Teach us, in all things, to trust in you without fear. Amen.

27

A Brand New Shiny Life
The Novelty of It All

"Arise, my love, my fair one, and come away;
for now the winter is past, the rain is over and
gone. The flowers appear on the earth; the
time of singing has come...."

— Song of Songs 2:10–12a

However cold the Russian winter, it was over, at least for Masha. Arriving at the baby house one day after our court appearance to begin the long journey home, we were ushered very quickly into a small hallway. Masha was told to undress. She was so skinny that we could count all her ribs and every bone in her spine. The dress she had worn, the underwear, socks, and shoes were given back to the orphanage. Taking out the clothes we had brought for her, we realized that even though they were only a toddler size two, they were still a bit big. It may have been the first time Masha wore pants. Not knowing what size shoe she wore, we brought three different pairs. The smallest ones, brown leather moccasin boots, fit best. Reluctantly, she left her turquoise shoes behind. There was nothing for her to take with her, except the musical toy and the photo album we had given her. Everything she owned had come from us.

There was little time for good-byes, as we were headed directly to the airport to catch the next flight to Moscow. Putting on her new coat and hat, Masha waved as if she was going out to play. She did not seem to understand that she would never return. The other children her age, including Olya and Valentina, were seated at little tables for dinner. Masha stood with us in the doorway waving and saying *"Pa-ka, pa-ka,"* Russian for "bye-bye." She said it so insistently that it seemed to me that she had longed for this moment with all her being. The other children responded with waves and *pa-ka's* too. I could see the caregivers' eyes well up with tears. It was hard to tell just whom they were crying for: Masha, the children left behind, or themselves.

The director was waiting for us outside. Alla told Masha how beautiful she looked and how nice her new coat was. Scooping her up, she spun Masha around on the walkway. They hugged and laughed together. Alla repeated all her previous instructions about listening and being good. Handing us Masha's medical records, she pulled out a small plastic cross on a ribbon on which Masha's name was handwritten in Cyrillic. Alla explained that she had called a local Orthodox priest to baptize the children at the orphanage. He had given these little crosses to them as proof of their sacramental grace. Turning toward us intently, she advised that it would be best if we encouraged Masha to forget everything about her life in Russia. She told us it was better for the children to forget the unhappy times of their lives if they could. Of course, that is the BIG if!

Suddenly, Masha was exposed to the world outside the orphanage. That world was very much bigger than she had thought. Everything we did was new and strange. Cars, planes, foods, beds, toilets—nothing was the same. There was far too much to take in all at once. As a result, Masha was on constant overload. She needed a great deal of reassurance. We were grateful that we had learned enough Russian to speak to an almost three-year-old, and I was surprised that so much of my one year of college Russian actually came back to me. But most college language courses don't teach their students how to ask a child if she has to go potty, and the words common to Russian literature, like "predestination" and the verb "to-shoot-oneself," were not particularly relevant.

Those first few days together in Moscow were filled with discovery for Masha and for us. Masha was delighted to go shopping, and all the clerks loved her. A street vendor was so enchanted by her that he gave her a small *matryoshka,* or stacking wooden doll.

Masha danced with abandon in the streets of Moscow, singing a little nursery rhyme as she went and holding tightly onto my hand. At McDonald's she winced at the ice in her drink, tore the breading off her chicken nuggets, and had no use for fries. (My, how things change!) On the other hand, she couldn't get enough yogurt or eat too many apples. On one occasion, we ordered soup from room service, figuring that it would be familiar to her. Masha promptly fished everything out of the soup, and ate only the broth. We wondered if that had been all the orphanage had had to give her.

In the process of sizing one another up, we were able to glimpse some of Masha's emotional turmoil. At one point, she dropped and broke a glass on the hotel room floor. Immediately, she flew into such a hysterical panic that it was hard to tell which was more shattered—the glass or the child. She seemed terrified that we would punish her. In retrospect, I think she was worried that we might send her back to the orphanage for causing such an accident. We quickly reassured her that she was going "home," despite the fact that she had no concept of what home was.

Masha was friendly and generally well mannered, but at times she was hard to settle down. Within a few days she began testing our limits, and stood up to me when I told her that she couldn't eat candy for supper. Repeating my instruction, she tried to get her way by manipulating me with smiles, giggles, and hugs. She was extremely frustrated to find that her technique didn't work!

Masha tried this form of manipulation a lot. During our time in Moscow, she tested our commitment to the rule of law on almost every issue involving parental authority. As tempting as it was to feel sorry for her and cave in, we stood firm. In all honesty, I was afraid not to. By the end of each day, I felt completely depleted. Fortunately, because life outside the orphanage was emotionally exhausting for Masha, getting her to bed generally wasn't too difficult, although she preferred to see us sleeping alongside her bed—a duty I, for one, was only too happy to assume! Part of her bedtime ritual, however, involved frantic rocking back and forth in an attempt to soothe herself; clearly, this child had been deeply hurt.

Newly adopted children are a cross between bulls in a china shop and kids on Christmas morning. Everything stimulates them, everything excites them, and everything exhausts them. New parents can't help but follow the same pattern. Because lots of changes are being made in quick succession, there is a tendency to try to do everything at once. The work of learning to love and live with one another, however, takes time.

In the early days of being a family, it may be best to keep stress as minimal as possible. While everyone wants to meet your new son or daughter, they do not all need to rush into your child's life at once. It is important

for us to remember that in coming home our children have also had to leave some things behind. While we may be on cloud nine, the recently adopted child may feel as if he is falling out of the sky. We just need to open our hearts wide enough to catch him.

New love is a springtime in its own right. A new child in the family is reason to celebrate with joy. The "issues" we observe in those early days can wait. It won't be long until the challenges present themselves; adoptive parents do not need to search them out. We only need to observe and respond.

God celebrates each of us. The warm breath of the divine Spirit melts the winter of our icy souls. Our Father's presence is the seal of hope and the promise of new life. Coming away with the Lord, the rains end, the sun rises, and flowers appear. The deserts we have known burst into bloom. Our Father knows that the pain we experience in spiritual growth will come soon enough. The moment God first grasps us as his own is precious to him. It is a time for singing. And if we listen, we may even hear the sound of God's voice in the song.

Holy Spirit, Everlasting Spring, you make everything new. In you all things come to color and life. Teach us to be fully present to the moment. Inspire us to discover one another, to unwrap the gift of being family. Help us to leave progress for

another day. Give us joy in the miracle we have received, in promises made and fulfilled, in the journey's end that turns to new beginnings. Melt the winters our children have endured. Bring our hearts to singing and our souls to laughter. Keep the memory of these early days alive in us that we may draw strength from them as we learn to live and love together. Amen.

28

Settling In
Rules and Realities

> "You have seen what I did to the Egyptians, and how I bore you on eagles' wings and brought you to myself. Now therefore, if you obey my voice and keep my covenant, you shall be my treasured possession out of all the peoples."
>
> — Exodus 19:4–5a

When our family met us at the airport shuttle bus station, Masha recognized them from the little photo album she carried around. In the few weeks since we had first met her, our new Russian daughter had learned all of her brothers' and sisters' names. Meanwhile, our other kids had seen photos and videos we had taken of Masha on our first trip. She went from one child to the next saying hello in Russian and pronouncing each of their names. Watching the whole thing come to life for all of them was pure delight!

Masha quickly found that her new home had some things in common with the only other "home" she remembered. The baby house was situated in the middle of a forest through which the train to Moscow travels. Our house is right next to the town conservation land, and we can see the commuter rail as it passes nearby. And there were lots of children, accompanied by lots of noise—perhaps not as much noise as 120 children can make, but on some days it might have been hard to tell the difference! I imagine that arriving at our house must have seemed to Masha a lot like moving to a fancier orphanage with better food. With five girls sharing a big bedroom, there was certainly a basis for some confusion.

There were, however, an overwhelming number of changes for our new daughter to adjust to. The most dramatic perhaps was the concept of freedom. Masha had never actually been allowed to decide anything. The expectations of the orphanage caregivers were clear. There was little spontaneity in play or in relationships. Everything was organized and supervised. Nothing was left to chance. She was told when to go, where to go, and what to do when she got there. Mostly, she was led by the hand. Eventually, she was even told to go with strangers she hardly knew to the opposite side of the globe.

Very early on, we observed that Masha did not know what to do with the freedom our other children exercised without thinking. It perplexed her so much that when offered a choice, she would become so dazed that she could not make one. A question like, "What would you like to eat?" didn't make any sense to her. I found that all I could do was give her an either-or proposition. "Do you want cheese or bread?" (Usually, the answer was a banana. On one day, she actually ate nine of them!)

Masha soon figured out that when she asked for something she would get it. Suddenly, there was no end to her asking. All she wanted to do was have whatever she desired, simply because, for the first time in her life, she could. Masha would frequently have several plates of different foods lined up in front of her chair. She didn't eat many of them. She just wanted to exercise her options. After a while, we exercised ours.

The concept of personal property was completely foreign to Masha as well. This placed a particular strain on her relationships with her brothers and sisters. Because nothing had been hers before, Masha was quick to say that *everything* she saw belonged to her alone. Our other children were not at all happy to hear the Russian word for "mine" sweepingly applied to things that belonged to them. Masha did not know how to distinguish between what was communal property and what belonged to individuals in the house. Try as we did, there was no simple way to explain it. As a result, she got herself into big trouble with her older sister by "playing" with her Madeline dollhouse. We rescued a few dolls from the toilet bowl and put all the furniture back together. After a few rather difficult incidents, she—and her younger partner in crime—knew better and did better.

While we expected to encounter substantial adjustment issues, there were things missing from Masha's orphanage life that had never crossed our minds. She had never been in a kitchen, never ridden in a car, never seen anything bought or sold. Because her diet was so poor, Masha did not know what most fruits and vegetables were. She had never encountered many of them. To keep the children safe, the orphanage silverware was limited to spoons. Masha had never even seen a fork. For months after coming home she couldn't remember what to call it. She had heard a lot of crying babies all her life, and had never been alone. She had felt hungry night after night when she went to bed, but didn't really know how to ask for food. On the other hand, she knew just what to do to steer a little attention in her direction when she wanted it—cuddles, kisses, and smiles may have been how she got more attention than other children at the orphanage. She also knew how to fly at altitudes well below adult radar. In short, Masha knew a lot about how to survive, but not very much about how to simply live. Inculturating her to daily life in a family setting was obviously going to take time.

It does not take long for adoptive parents to figure out that they need to adjust almost as much as their new child. In truth, every family member will adapt not only to the newest addition, but also to the new dynamic that arises. This process is often slower than we would like it to be. It calls for more patience and work than we might expect.

The most challenging thing for new families to establish is discipline. While most children we adopt have lived in an environment with rules and routines, many have little appreciation for parental authority. The adopted child's experience is largely limited to rules without relationship. Rules are made and enforced by whoever is "in power." Genuine authority, however, is personal. It can exist only in the context of an ongoing relationship. An adoptive family may be the first stable set of interpersonal relationships some children have ever had. The stronger those relationships become, the more secure a child will feel. A child who trusts is able to accept authority.

God rescued the children of Israel from slavery in Egypt. Empowering Moses to lead them, the Almighty brought his people to himself. Borne up on eagle's wings, they breathed the air of freedom for the first time in generations. Their Father gave them everything in advance. Only then did the Holy One ask them to obey his voice and keep the covenant. If they chose to accept divine authority, they would be God's most treasured possession.

Adoption offers us the opportunity to act the way God did all those centuries ago. You will carry your daughter home with strong arms, delivering her to a land of promise flowing with the milk and honey of unconditional love. You will give yourself to your son long before he decides whether he will give himself to you.

Our heavenly Father gives everything to us before he asks anything of us. God's commandments are always given in the context of an ongoing and personal relationship. The Lord frees us for freedom. Reminding us of all that has been done on our behalf, God's Holy Spirit waits for us to ask what we might do in return.

Holy Spirit, Spirit of Freedom, write your law in our hearts. Show us how to be truly free. Help us to love what is good and right. Empower us to make choices according to your will. Teach us how to use authority well: to establish rules for the sake of relationships and to inspire mutual respect in our home. Guide our children toward security and trust. Help them to know that we will be faithful to them, that we will keep our word. Show us the adjustments we must make. Enable us to give ourselves fully to our children without the expectation of receiving their love in return. Amen.

29

Being There

Building Trust and the Gift of Presence

"I will be with you; I will not fail you or forsake you."

— Joshua 1:5b

*M*asha stuck to me like Velcro soaked in super-glue and set in concrete. She followed me everywhere, at times so closely that I knocked her down just by turning around. I was the object of her every waking moment. She was more cautious with Andrew. But in a pinch, even he would do. Because all the orphanage workers were women, men were just one of those things she had to get used to. (I'm not sure I've completely adjusted to them!)

Though she was all smiles, it was evident that Masha had a real fear of abandonment. Any time I left the house, she demanded reassurance that I would return. She maintained an unwavering surveillance of the front door. Every time I got near it, she required a hug and a kiss—even when I was just walking down to the end of the driveway to get the mail. There was no such thing as giving Masha the slip—she always knew who was home and who wasn't. When anyone did come home, Masha was the very first to greet them at the door. She still is.

Separation anxiety influenced a great deal of Masha's behavior. It was the "man behind the curtain" whenever her Wizard of Oz appeared. What Masha did was not particularly immature, but the way she did things revealed what an insecure child she was. Masha did not know how to relax. Her muscles were always tense. She rushed into and out of just about every activity frantically, even frenetically at times. She had three-year-old ideas, but the discipline level of a one-year-old. Above all, Masha worried perpetually. It seemed as though she was afraid that someday she would wake up and find that coming home had only been a dream.

Masha was determined to hold on to her new life with every bit of strength she had. She was far too scared to let go. Fear permeated her family relationships in those early weeks. It showed its face in unyielding perfectionism. If she made a mistake, Masha was devastated. She simply could not trust that we would love her in spite of it. Crying over spilt milk was not at all an exaggeration. Actually, it took a lot less than that to make her cry. The Russian words I used most often were *"nee nada plachat,"* "there's no need to cry." The potential consequences of imperfection were not something Masha was willing to risk. The power of her anxiety was so strong that at times she even lied to us.

Winston Churchill once called Russia "a riddle wrapped in a mystery inside an enigma." That daunting description wasn't far from how I saw Masha's behavior, at least in the beginning. Trying to figure her out was functionally impossible. Much of how she acted was odd; a good deal of it seemed quite irrational. I started to make headway only when I realized that Masha was probably doing what all of us do: acting out of her own life experience. I couldn't understand how the past was shaping her actions, because I had not been a part of it. I hadn't been there with her.

No matter how experienced you are in childraising, there are some discipline techniques that may not work well with your newly adopted child. As a mother of seven children already, I was not at all prepared to completely retool my skills for number eight. I was certainly not willing to let our daughter make a transition from "poor orphan" to "spoiled brat." But seeing her fear of rejection and abandonment, I knew that things like "time out" were not at all appropriate. The last thing Masha needed was to be sent away alone.

Other methods don't offer the adoptive parent much help either. Spanking, even in moderation, is not a real option. Any child with a history of abuse cannot be taught by what may have, at another time, threatened his life. Depending on a child's pre-adoption background, even raising your voice can be destructive to long term parenting goals. (That, in particular, has been very challenging for me.) Simply stated, deprivation doesn't work. A child who has had so little of what she needs is unlikely to be swayed by whatever you might take away from her. What, after all, can anyone take away from a child who at one time did not have a family? The truth is that most standard approaches to discipline undermine the trust that your child needs to build.

The answer is for parents to become creative and a little unconventional. What we have found is that just being there goes a long, long way. The best thing to do with bad behavior is to use it to reinforce, rather than threaten, family relationships. Taking Masha in my arms and looking her in the eye, I calmly, but firmly, correct her. My temper doesn't make it easy for me to discipline in that way. But when I have been able to muster it, I have been far more successful. It even works with our other kids!

Presence is the key to breaking the code of a child's behavior. It is the only way to heal the absences of the past that are so deep they can still be felt. Presence, in fact, is what draws our children out of their painful or disrupted pasts. In presence, our children begin to trust. In trust, they reach out to the future.

We give our children so many things. All of what they need and much of what they desire come as the result of our love for them. But if all that we have given them were to be lost, they would still have what they need most. They would have us. Ultimately, what our children want more than anything else is simply our presence. They want us to watch them, to hear them, to touch them. There is no mystery in that. It is because, like the rest of us, they want to be seen, heard, and touched.

God created us to be with him and with others. Our whole lives are really one extended opportunity for presence with one another and with him. That is why our Father continually gives us the assurance of his presence. The Holy Spirit does not fail us because he does not forsake us. The divine Spirit of adoption is the One sent to fulfill the promise Jesus made to his disciples when he said, "I will not leave you orphaned" (Jn 14:18).

All that we possess comes from God. But beyond what he has given us remains God himself. The divine Giver wishes, more than anything else, to give us his own life. Never abandoning us, God's presence heals the hurts each of us has suffered. Holding us in a mystical embrace, our heavenly Father teaches us to trust in his abiding love.

Holy Spirit, Divine Presence, you have never failed or abandoned us. Help us to experience your abiding love, to sense that you are always with us, always for us, always among us, even within us. Show us how to be truly and actively present to our children. Teach us to watch them, to listen to them, and to touch them. Keep us from trying to substitute other things for our presence in their lives. Give us the answers to questions we never even imagined. Inspire creative approaches to challenging behavior. Enable our children to accept our presence in their lives. Inspire in their young hearts, and ours, fresh hope for the future. Amen.

30

Bonding and Attachment
Love's Two-Way Street

> Yet it was I who taught Ephraim to walk, I took
> them up in my arms; but they did not know
> that I healed them. I led them with cords of
> human kindness, with bands of love. I was to
> them like those who lift infants to their
> cheeks. I bent down to feed them.
>
> — Hosea 11:3–4

*M*ary may have had a little lamb, but we had
Masha. She followed us everywhere, from room to
room, upstairs and down, from chair to couch and
back. No one could get rid of her, not even by going to
the bathroom! Masha was unbearably clingy. We knew
that bonding would take time, but we didn't expect that
it would be so aggravating. While we appreciated
Masha's affection, we wished that it would come in

smaller doses. There were plenty of times I just wanted to push her away. Sometimes, I did.

There were other instances, however, when Masha pulled away from me. She had an amazing capacity to look in every direction other than mine when she didn't like what I was telling her. If I demanded eye contact, she simply closed her eyes, and poof—I disappeared! Masha wanted and needed a lot of physical affection. She demanded it constantly. We began to notice, however, that she only accepted affection on her terms. When she asked to be held, she was happy. If I picked her up, she squirmed.

One of the most startling things about Masha was how she interacted with people. She had no sense of how intimate a relationship was or should be. Anyone who came through the door was fair game for anything. It didn't matter whether a person was a relative, a family friend, or a plumber. Masha was there in a flash, ready to throw herself at them. She was indiscriminate—and inappropriate—with her affection. I knew that something had to give when Masha ran up to a Home Depot employee and hugged him around the legs. Sure, the sinks were nice, but not that nice! An incident like that would cause any girl's mother to worry about how she would conduct herself later in life. Clearly, boundaries would have to be set and respected.

It was difficult to teach Masha what was appropriate because most of the adults she flirted with welcomed the attention she gave them. I tried to rein her in by telling them how unsafe it was for her to be so trusting of strangers. Most just responded by introducing themselves. Of course, that didn't solve anything. What finally worked was coming up with a way for Masha to physically connect with people she met, but at an acceptable level. When the instruction finally sank in, Masha learned to give the most enthusiastic handshakes ever!

Bonding is a process that is undertaken by every family member. Babies begin to bond to their parents even before birth. Sounds, warmth, nurturing, and all kind of physical sensations work together to establish a lasting connection between children and their parents. Newborns respond to the voices of their mothers and fathers. Brothers and sisters cuddle and play, interacting with familiarity and delight. Grandparents ooh and ah, hold and caress and "spoil" their grandchildren with attention. We all learn the meaning of intimacy through experience. Little by little, day after day, people become attached to one another by bonds meant to last a lifetime.

The ability to bond makes it possible for us to both give and receive love. Difficulties arise when the natural process of bonding is disrupted or incomplete. That is why healthy attachment is not a given for the adoptive child. Bonding is strengthened whenever a child has a need, expresses that need, and has it filled by a loving adult. When needs are unexpressed or unmet, the cycle is broken. A child's attachments are considered problematic when they are either too exclusive or not exclusive enough. The little boy who treats a bank teller the same way he treats his mother may have difficulty developing intimate relationships later on in life. A girl who will not let anyone but her mother touch her may experience the world as a lonely place full of strangers.

Love is often a response to love. Adoptive parents should expect to "front" a tremendous amount of love and affection for their new son or daughter, without anticipating an immediate return. Every child must be given reason to believe that his family is completely committed to him personally. Eye contact, physical touch, sweets, and even bottle-feeding have been helpful tools for families seeking to aid the bonding process.

While an adoption decree grants custody and legal responsibility, it cannot create personal attachments. There is no getting around the fact that adoptive parents and their children start out as strangers. To the extent that they bond to one another, they become a family.

God's whole purpose for our lives has to do with bonding. Our heavenly Father is completely attached to us. His greatest desire is for us to choose intimacy with him. All the love we have ever experienced comes from the Creator, so much so, in fact, that we can say that wherever love is, there is God.

Whether we know it or not, God has loved us from the start. It was the Lord who taught us to walk. It was the Father who took us in his arms to heal us when we were hurt. We moved along paths led by divine kindness. Never directionless, the Eternal drew us on with bands of love. When we were hungry, God bent down to feed us. When we were low, our heavenly Father lifted us up to the radiance of his face.

Not every child is grateful for her adoption. Likewise, not all of us have responded to God's love with love in return. Refusing to call God our Father, many have turned from following his Sprit. Set among his children, some have simply chosen to remain alone. God has experienced the disappointment of unrequited love. The prophet Jeremiah put it this way: "I thought how I would set you among my children, and give you a pleasant land, the most beautiful heritage of all the nations. And I thought you would call me, my Father, and would not turn from following me" (Jer 3:19). Still, there is always hope in heaven. For as long as the Father continues to love us as children, we may yet bond our hearts to his. Belonging to the Lord, we will find that the Holy One has been ours all along.

Holy Spirit, Spirit of Belonging, draw our hearts toward one another in love. Enable us to act tenderly, even

when it is inconvenient. Help us to recognize our children's need for affection. Show us how to use everything in our lives to grow in intimacy. Keep us from pushing our children away. Guide us, and them, in drawing healthy boundaries and attachments. Make us a family bound by love, conscious of one another's needs and desires. Give our children the grace to receive love and then to be able to give love in return. Lead us all by your kindness, and raise every one of us to the Father's face. Amen.

31

Traveling Heavy
Emotional Baggage

I have calmed and quieted my soul, like a
weaned child with its mother; my soul is like
the weaned child that is with me.
— Psalm 131:2

$\mathcal{W}$hen we left the orphanage, all we were allowed
to take with us was Masha. Because we had no delu-
sions about being fashionable, we traveled to Russia
with as little baggage as possible. At least, that is what
we thought. As it turned out, however, we discovered
that Masha had more luggage than we did. Neither of
us could see what she was carrying, but we could tell
that it was pretty heavy.

Masha wasn't exactly a crybaby, but she did an
awful lot of crying. It didn't take much to set her off.
Being caught with her hand in the cookie jar would

have provided at least some real reason. Sometimes it seemed as if anything could serve as a pretext for Masha's tears. If she fell down, Masha cried as if every bone in her body had been broken. If she was told to finish her supper, she bawled as if she hadn't eaten for days. If Masha didn't get my perpetual and undivided attention, she wept as if I had left her for hours.

Masha's moods were like tides. Suddenly and without warning, she could be subject to a wave of emotion so strong that it would carry her out to sea beyond our grasp. Sometimes we felt as if all we could do was stand on the beach, throw her a line, and hope to pull her back to shore. It was clear that beneath the surface, our daughter was dealing with a constant undercurrent of emotional distress.

At times Masha's behavior seemed odd and irrational. While I had spoken to her exclusively in Russian for the first few weeks at home, she was terrified if anyone else spoke Russian to her. When we met a friendly woman from St. Petersburg, Masha completely shut down. Refusing to respond, she wouldn't even look at her. We had been told by one of the agency workers that this was fairly typical behavior—that sometimes children are afraid that Russian-speakers might take them back to the orphanage. We found that our daughter was also quite a pack rat. She stashed cookies, raisins, meat sticks, candies, cheese, juice boxes—you name it—in dresser drawers, the girls' room closet, and innumerable bags and purses. She needed reassurance that she did not have to hoard food, that there would be enough, that it would not just disappear. The strangest thing of all was Masha's reaction to a bath towel. While she absolutely loved to be bathed, she was afraid of being wrapped in a bath towel to dry off. The first and only time I did it, she burst into tears and collapsed into a heap on the tile floor. What past trauma caused her to react in this way? We'll never really know—but we knew enough not to try it again.

There were aspects of Masha's behavior that really puzzled me. Because I couldn't figure out why she acted in certain ways, I had no clue about what to do or how to help her. For a while, I could only be a concerned bystander. But as I observed Masha more and more, I understood that she was simply trying to unpack her bags. Our job was to help her sort through what she had brought with her. In time, perhaps, we could encourage her to get rid of a few things.

All of us carry our emotional baggage with us. Burdens we pick up over the course of our lives are not easily laid down. Sometimes we are afraid to let go of them, because if we do we won't have anything to hang on to at all.

Adoptive children come with a whole set of luggage, some of it their own, some of it passed on to them by others. Children experience their emotional distress differently. Some feel the strain of carrying it quickly and all at once. Others become conscious of it only after years of dragging it around.

While none of us want to see our children's pain, it is important for adoptive parents to know that their child's emotional needs provide an opportunity for bonding. Your children's inner struggles cannot be magically fixed overnight. With patience and sensitivity, however, you will not only help them face what hurts, you will be there to face it with them.

God did not deliver the Israelites from bondage in order to abandon them in the desert. The God of Abraham, Isaac, and Jacob called their children out of Egypt to make them a chosen people all his own. Moses was the outstretched arm of God. Through his anointed agent of redemption, God brought Israel forth with mighty acts of power. The Lord freed them from slavery, from all the burdens they had borne in bondage. The Book of Exodus recounts God's plan: "I am the LORD, and I will free you from the burdens of the Egyptians and deliver you from slavery to them. I will redeem you with an outstretched arm and with mighty acts of judgment. I will take you as my people, and I will be your God" (6:6–7).

Yet, as difficult as it was to take the Israelites out of Egypt, it was even harder to take Egypt out of the Israelites. For forty years they wandered, still nostalgic for the security they left behind and the onions that grew along the Nile. Only afterward were they prepared to inherit what had been promised to them from the beginning.

Contentment is the gift of a peaceful spirit. As parents we know that one of the best things we can hope for our children is that they make enough peace with their lives to find peace in their hearts. The image of the weaned child sitting calmly on his mother's knee captures the essence of that hope. A child fully nurtured is a child fully at rest.

Most of our adoptive children are anything but calm, at least in the beginning. Their souls are scattered, not collected. Their hearts are restless rather than quiet. While we may want to focus our energy on weaning them from the past, we ought to understand that many of our children have had far too little time "at the breast." A child can only be weaned after he or she has been adequately nurtured.

Our God is not only a Father who delivers us, but also a Mother who nurtures us. The Lord offers each of us a strong arm and a tender breast. The Holy Spirit frees us from the burdens we carry. Leading us out of bondage and distress, God feeds us with the milk of divine presence.

Holy Spirit, Spirit of Grace and Prayer, we come to you for strength and comfort. Help us to go gently with one another. Show us how to lighten the burdens our children carry. Teach us how to weather the storms in their souls. Guide us in riding the waves and calming the winds that blow hard against them. Give us the wisdom to know when to be firm and when to be flexible. Fill us with sensitivity and patience. Empower us to face our children's hurts with them. Free us all from the heavy loads we bear, transform them into vehicles of your grace alive in us. Nurture us to contentment and bring our hearts to rest. Amen.

32

Healing Love

Fully Accepting Your Child

> But to all who received him, who believed in
> his name, he gave power to become chil-
> dren of God, who were born, not of blood or
> of the will of the flesh or the will of man, but of
> God.
>
> — John 1:12,13

The truth is that we didn't know how to handle Masha at times. It was difficult to find a way to accept her without validating behavior that was not at all acceptable. Masha desperately wanted to fit in and be good; she just didn't know how. Struggling to come up with a winning strategy, it became apparent that normal everyday childraising was more than she could take. When I'd try to correct her, I often ended up crushing her. Masha wasn't really able to take much of anything in stride. She had been deeply wounded.

I was more than willing to accept Masha's background. In retrospect, though, I realize that I was a lot less willing to accept the damage her past had caused her. The actual neglect she had suffered was behind her. The fact that she continued to be affected by it—well, that was another matter. It took a while for us to understand that although we had expected scars, Masha still had open wounds. None of the band-aids in our medicine cabinet were the right size. And even if they had been, we didn't have nearly enough of them.

After several months had passed, we had resigned ourselves to muddling through whatever our daughter presented to us. On one particularly challenging day, however, everything changed. For most of the morning it had seemed that Masha's emotional kettle was about to boil over. After correcting yet another misbehavior, I picked our daughter up and cradled her. Within minutes Masha's floodgates opened. She cried so hard that I shuddered at what anyone would think if they heard her. For more than twenty minutes Masha sobbed. Her cries were not like anything I had ever heard—even from her. They came from the core of her being, from the pit of human suffering. When she finally stopped, Masha calmed down. Exhausted, she fell asleep.

Every day for the next few weeks, Masha asked to be held. Taking our daughter in my arms, I encouraged her to cry out her grief. At times, we cried right along with her. Evidently, Masha had a lot to cry about.

Reflecting on what I knew about her short life, I realized that most of what had happened to her gave her reason enough.

After some time, Masha cried less and talked more. Recounting incidents from her past, she described rooms and faces and events in vivid detail. Even though some of what she talked about seemed to predate her time in the orphanage, it was as fresh to her as the present moment. More than simply remembering her past, Masha was reliving it. As memories flooded into her mind, tears ran down her cheeks. These tears were not ordinary in any way. They were old tears, healing tears. She had stored them up until she felt safe enough to release them. I count them as precious as any gift I have ever received.

Accepting a child means accepting all that has wounded him. Parents should be prepared to recognize that some of the behaviors they'd like to change flow from the hurts their children have suffered. Hardest to accept, I think, are the injuries we have had nothing to do with, the hurts that others have caused. While it is tempting to sweep a child's woundedness under the rug, or trust that time will heal all, it is far better to accept the full force of our children's past hurts. Enduring pain is not the same as accepting it. If presence leads to trust, acceptance gives hope for healing.

When we fully accept our children as they are, we free them to become more fully themselves. Once brought into the light, the injuries we sustain can become secret passageways to our deepest fulfillment. The little boy who knows loneliness becomes a loyal friend. The girl who understands rejection welcomes others without reservation. Children who have lived in fear become pillars of strength and consolation. Drawing on the wounds we bear, we become better than whole.

Not every hurt can be healed completely. But those that linger in the children we love stretch our hearts more broadly and more deeply. If children teach us anything, they teach us to love past the horizon and beyond the shallows. After all is said and done, adoption is a vehicle of healing love.

Power to be in relationship flows both from receiving and believing. In receiving the Son, we come into relationship with the divine Being. We receive God's receiving of us. The Lord gives us power to become his children. That power is more than birth, or blood, or the human will can attain. It is the force of the very will of God that makes it possible for us to believe.

When we accept a child as she is, one "such as this," we welcome Christ himself. The words of Jesus echo through the Gospel: "Anyone who welcomes one such child in my name, welcomes me" (Mt 18:5). There is no greater blessing adoption can bring to us. The truly wonderful thing, however, is greater still. When our children so willingly accept us as we are, they give us the healing love we need. In us, they encounter the very same Jesus we welcome in them.

Holy Spirit, Spirit of Welcome, you do not reject anyone who comes to you. Help us to receive one another as we are. Show us how to fully accept our children the way they have come to us. Teach us to love them unconditionally and without reserve. Open our hearts to their wounds. Help us to listen to their pain and share it. Guide our children through their grief. Give us all the gift of tears that heal. Transform our injuries into victories, and our hurts into gifts. Sustain us in hope. Empower us to believe. Through the love you have inspired, heal us all. Amen.

33

No News or Good News?
Family Matter vs.
Public Announcement

"Which one of you having a hundred sheep
and losing one of them, does not leave the
ninety-nine in the wilderness and go after the
one that is lost until he finds it? When he has
found it, he lays it on his shoulders and rejoic-
es. And when he comes home, he calls
together his neighbors, saying to them,
'Rejoice with me, for I have found my sheep
that was lost.'"

— Luke 15:4

*B*efore we even brought Masha home, all of our
friends and relatives, and most of the people we dealt
with on a daily basis, knew that we were in the midst of
adopting a child. Those who were a real part of our
lives expressed interest in how the process worked or

what was next on our to-do list. Some were intrigued with how we came to the decision to adopt. Others shared how they had toyed with the idea of adopting a child themselves. As things moved forward, I answered most of the questions people asked. Mostly, their questions were heartfelt and innocuous.

There was, however, a completely other class of people who were downright nosey. While they were not a regular part of our lives, they had no trouble asking the most intimate questions. One woman inquired as to what our adoption was going to cost. Hey, I told her, other people redo their kitchens. Another asked explicitly about Masha's background and her "real" mother. I went into a discourse on life in Russian orphanages and the economic crises that resulted from the fall of Soviet Communism.

Generally, we found ways to avoid answering questions that people should have known better than to ask. We also trained our other kids in the tactics of escape and evasion, that is, how to recognize an inappropriate question and how to keep from answering any that fell into the all-you-ever-wanted-to-know-about-my-adopted-sister-and-were-brazen-enough-to-ask category. We discovered that the best way to prevent the kids from making a mistake was to keep them partially in the dark as well. Treating information on a need-to-know basis was very helpful indeed. Even they didn't need to know every detail of Masha's past.

We didn't throw a "coming out" party for Masha when she came home. At twenty-two pounds, she wouldn't have made much of an impression as a debutante! While all our friends wanted to meet Masha and make her feel welcome, they gave us all the space we needed. Many of them caught up with all of us at church on Sunday morning, or stopped by for a brief visit at our house. In those early weeks, we kept things as uncomplicated as possible. We celebrated Masha's third birthday and her Baptism, but not anything that was peculiar to her adoption.

We filed for a state adoption decree about a year and a half later, a procedure necessary in order to obtain a U.S. birth certificate for Masha. Calling our day in court "adoption day," we decided to make it a joyous occasion for the whole family. I bought Masha and her younger sister fancy new dresses. We pulled the rest of our kids out of school so that everyone could be there. We took grandparents, great-grandparents, godparents, and even a priest along, and brought along bread and salt, traditional foods of Russian hospitality, to share with the judge. The priest performed the "Order for the Blessing of Parents and an Adopted Child," from the *Book of Blessings*, in the courthouse atrium. Masha was so excited that she told everyone at preschool. Most of the kids didn't have a clue what she was talking about. Her teacher, however, couldn't have been happier. She had adopted children herself.

Adoption is part of our family's history, but mostly, it belongs to Masha. She, after all, is the only one to have experienced life on both sides of that watershed event. Respecting Masha's right to tell her own story is something we consider critically important. That is why I have chosen not to use our daughter's real name in this book. When people ask if our two youngest daughters are twins, I usually tell them that one child is biological and one is adoptive. I never tell them which one is which. If they insist, I invite them to guess. They almost always get it wrong.

Parents have very different opinions about who and how much to tell about their child's adoption. Some make their family history a kind of public scrapbook. Others guard their child's adoption as a family matter. A child adopted in infancy will need time to understand the role of adoption in his own life. A child who is older at the time of her adoption may need to grieve what has been lost from a former life. And, while it is increasingly rare, some children do not know that their parents are adoptive rather than biological.

While we haven't hidden the fact that Masha came to us through adoption, we haven't made it a primary topic of discussion either. Adoption just doesn't seem to follow naturally from a conversation about the weather. Our goal has been to treat adoption as if it is normal—and, believe it or not, it actually is. In that regard, nonchalance goes a long way. "Oh, you're from Russia? That's nice, dear."

That being said, not every family has a choice. "Obviously" adoptive families tend to attract busybodies. It seems that racial and cultural differences make some people think they have a right to ask the details of a person's life story. It is possible to fend them off without being too rude. Often, a good sense of humor is the best defense.

No matter where you stand on the matter, the same basic principle applies: not everything is everyone's business. Those who share information should tell their stories without any pressure. Those who withhold information should do so without feeling any shame. However you choose to handle information about your child's adoption, you ought to handle it with and not just for your child.

The adoptive family may find it helpful to reflect on the difference between private and personal. An adoption cannot be purely private as it is a matter of public record and civic courts. Adoption is undoubtedly, however, an intensely personal affair. We often forget that personal means having to do with a person; a real human being who belongs, as we all do, to the family of humanity. As parents, our prime concern should be maintaining the dignity of our children as people.

Our Master has many sheep. Each and every one of them is uniquely precious and irreplaceable. When one is missing, our Lord leaves the rest of the flock behind to find it. The divine Shepherd scours the wilderness. Searching every cave and canyon, the Holy One refuses to return empty-handed. When the Shepherd has found what is lost, he carries it in his arms. Arriving home, he announces the good news. God cannot contain himself, for what was lost has been found. Together, all the host of heaven rejoice.

From God's point of view, human history reads like a sequence of lost and founds. Our Lord is one that seeks out the lost. At one time or another each of us falls into the pit of that category. God always knows where we are, even if we haven't quite figured out just how far we've wandered away. There is nothing our Father will not do to find us, no length to which he will not go to bring us home in his arms. All that belongs to heaven ultimately returns there. Our Father turns every losing into finding. We are the cause of God's joy.

Joy is meant to be shared and it multiplies in the sharing. Not every crevice and bramble needs to be recounted in the telling of our tales, for the heart of salvation's story does not change. Each of our lives testifies to the truth that all that is lost can be found. All that is missing can and will be restored. There is no greater cause for celebration.

Holy Spirit, Spirit bearing witness to our souls, help us to tell the story of your love with our lives more than with our words. Show us how to preserve our children's dignity.

Teach us to direct our joy. Keep us from volunteering too much information to those who do not need to know. Guide us in setting appropriate boundaries and help us to respect them. In celebrating our children's homecoming, give us discretion and modesty. Make us sensitive to our children's need for privacy and to their desire for intimacy. Amen.

34

Overshadowing Sadness
Post-Adoptive Depression

With weeping they shall come, and with consolations I will lead them back, I will let them
walk by brooks of water, in a straight path in
which they shall not stumble....

— Jeremiah 31:9a

$\mathcal{W}$hen I think about it, I had some pretty unrealistic expectations of myself in parenting our adopted
daughter. Given my maternal resume, I thought that I
would know exactly what to do. After raising so many
children, I doubted that I would be thrown any pitches
I had never seen before. Even if I couldn't hit them out
of the park, I felt certain that I would manage to get on
base at the very least.

Masha, however, was an entirely different ball
game, so to speak. She had the ability to keep us guess-

ing. Mostly, I did a lot of second-guessing my responses to her. Masha wasn't much different from what I expected her to be. My skills in handling her, however, most definitely were. After seven children, I felt a crisis of confidence. I felt as if I was striking out with her on a daily basis. The visiting team was definitely ahead. Even on our own field, it didn't seem as if being the captain of the home team gave me any advantage whatsoever. I was, without a doubt, my own worst umpire.

There were days I wondered if adopting any child had been a very big mistake. It wasn't that I didn't love Masha. Much to the contrary, my doubts surfaced *because* I loved her. I knew that Masha was worth the work. It's just that I felt unequal to what she needed. There was no turning back. The choices had already been made, and I had to find a way to live with them. Exhausted by my constant attempts to do it right, I wondered where I could turn for help or even consolation.

At the end of a particularly difficult day, I realized I didn't really have a problem with what our lives were actually like. Objectively, everything was going well. My discontent was rooted in the disjuncture between reality and my expectations. Living wasn't the issue; living up to was. Mostly, I had expected far too much of my highly honed maternal expertise. I felt exhausted, inadequate, and just plain down. I decided to let things go and stopped being so hard on myself. That kept me from being too hard on everyone else, at least some-what. Within a few weeks, Masha adjusted markedly, and my batting average improved.

Parents who feel sad and overwhelmed may find consolation in knowing that they are by no means alone. Though we may expect to be walking on air, neg-ative emotions shouldn't come as a surprise to us. Completing an adoption is not unlike getting married, buying a house, or caring for someone who is sick. Suddenly, the whirlwind stops. There is an unavoidable emotional let down after the flurry of the adoption process is over.

When a child comes home, the "goal" is accom-plished and the real work of parenting begins. That work can be rather mundane, repetitive, even boring. It can also be unrelenting, frustrating, or overwhelming. Whatever the case, parenting is the most demanding job on earth. Adoptive children are often especially needy, leaving parents with more of their own needs unmet.

New parents, who may have unwittingly romanti-cized family life, may not feel as fulfilled as they had hoped. Unfortunately, waiting patiently to have a child doesn't make raising one any easier. Constructing those idyllic Norman Rockwell-esque scenes we all imagine takes longer than we anticipated. Breaking them down, however, can be done in a matter of minutes, and find-ing out that they were merely paintings on a canvas, seconds. Suddenly, we find ourselves back at the easel with little motivation to paint much of anything at all.

Post-Adoptive Depression Syndrome (PADS) is very real. It is also relatively common. If you experience depression-like symptoms, you may profit from addressing your situation with a health professional. PADS does not mean that you love your children any less. Nor does PADS indicate that you are a bad or less-than-adequate parent. What it might mean is that you need to take the bull a bit less by the horns, and allow yourself more time to adjust to your new family responsibilities. Forget about the housekeeping and haute cuisine for a while. No one ever died from a few weeks with dust bunnies or frozen dinners.

God consoles us when we are overwhelmed and exhausted. The Holy Spirit is our Comforter, our help in times of distress. God does not help us from a distance. Our Father sends the Spirit to be with us and within us. That Spirit knows how hard we try, how bad we may feel, how hopeless things may look to us. God does not leave us, no matter what dark places of the soul our tears take us to. Gently, the Lifegiver brings us back. He guides us to the streams of divine presence. Allowing us to walk alongside the running waters, God sets our weary feet on a path straight and smooth, one on which we will not stumble.

If we come to our Father, we will find the rest we need and the comfort we desire. God's love does not change because of our shortcomings. Instead, the Lord reveals the depths of his love for us. There is no fault or inadequacy that God cannot help us to overcome. There is no reason for sadness, but if we feel sad anyway, God reaches out with consolations only the Holy One can give.

Holy Spirit, Source of Heavenly Water, overflow our souls. Protect us from discouragement and exhaustion. Fill us with hope when we are tempted to despair. Reassure us when we doubt. Guide our expectations and keep us from being too hard on others or on ourselves. Strengthen us when we are overwhelmed. Be with us in the midst of our struggles. In meeting the needs of our children, show us how to have our needs met as well. Set our feet on a smooth path and lift us when we stumble. Lead us and our children to the cool streams of your presence, and give us the consolation we need to go on. Amen.

35

The "Blended" Family
Biological and Adoptive Children Together

"I have other sheep that do not belong to this fold. I must bring them also, and they will listen to my voice. So there will be one flock and one shepherd."

— John 10:16

*B*elonging is a very hard thing to define. Part of how we come to own things is that they've been part of our lives over a period of time. Sometimes we attach significance to things because they were given to us by someone we care about, or on a special occasion we think is worth remembering. What we possess also possesses us. Something occurs at the level of identity when we think of something as belonging to us.

If what makes something ours is a tough concept to grasp, what makes someone ours is even more mysterious. Although she shared our last name and lived at our address, it took a while for me to feel as if Masha was mine. Even though we had a court decree stating that she belonged to us, to me it still felt as if Masha was someone else's child.

Initially, it seemed that way to our other kids too. Masha looked a lot like them. She had a personality that meshed well with the rest of theirs. But when Masha first came home, she was more of a guest than a sister. She wasn't quite one of the gang.

The pace of our household is very fast, probably much faster than those of our smaller family counterparts. Dinner table conversation doesn't just buzz, it sounds like the whole hive is swarming. In the early days, Masha just couldn't keep up. Most of her food was eaten after her brothers and sisters left the dining room. Because she so desperately wanted to be like the rest of the kids in the house, Masha never stopped trying to fit in. Often the results were less than positive. They were annoyed by her behavior, and she was overwhelmed by their expectations.

Part of what kept our kids feeling a bit separate was that they didn't speak the same language. But in those first few weeks, our kids learned almost as much Russian as Masha did English. They picked it up as quickly as she put it down. A virtual cultural exchange

took root, and our kids joined in when Masha decided
to sing her little nursery rhyme. While she was busy
becoming one of us, we all became a bit more like her.
Within a couple of months, our other kids knew more
Russian than Masha.

Russian, however, wasn't the only thing foreign
about how Masha communicated. The real difference
was in how our children interacted with each other.
Masha had no idea how to have a brother or to be a sister. While there were certainly enough other children
with her at the orphanage, relationships between the
children there had always been mediated by an adult.
Here, she had to find her place and learn how to hold
onto it.

Our family had fit together just fine before Masha
arrived. When she came, we realized that the puzzle of
household personalities would have to make room for
an entirely new and different piece. Trying to figure
out just where she fit in wasn't easy, especially when the
other pieces were disrupted. Sometimes it seemed as if
Masha was part of a whole different picture.

As parents, we found it very hard to treat our children, biological and adoptive, equally. At times, I
became obsessed with trying to be fair. Carefully watching my every move, I micromanaged who got the first
dish of ice cream and who got the first turn on the yel-
low swing. (I've never understood what was wrong with
the green one!) Because Masha was new to family life,

she needed—and demanded—a lot of extra attention. While our other kids were more than understanding, there were times when they got less from us than they deserved—less than they had been accustomed to receiving. While there wasn't any magic moment of inclusion, the children worked out their own pecking order and protocol in time. In the end, we saw that they really didn't need our assistance to figure it all out.

For parents of "blended families," impartiality must be the rule. While many may think that biological children are the natural beneficiaries of preferential treatment, often it is our adoptive children who end up with the biggest slice of the pie. In trying to be fair, parents should let go of the notion that they can be equal with their children. Kids have different needs. A piano costs more than a clarinet, and a shoe size twelve double E will take more time to find than a seven medium. Our adoptive child's needs may be more intense, at least for a while. Still, every child needs parents—those that we birth as well as those we adopt.

Feelings of affection for our children grow. Adoptive parents ought not to expect to feel the same love for a newly adopted son or daughter as they do for the children they already have. Disparity in this regard has nothing to do with birth. Mostly, it's all about time, or, more accurately, the lack of it. In time, the sparkle in your eye will shine more brightly. On a day in the not so distant future, you will notice that the affection you have for all your children is pretty much the same. In the meantime, bonding is strengthened when parents act "as if" they already feel the way they eventually will.

The flock of the Shepherd comes from many pastures. From all the grasslands, fields, and hills God calls each sheep by name. We may not recognize the sound of every bleat or the color and texture of every woolen coat. Still, all sheep know the voice of the Lord who calls them. Finally brought together—gathered in one place—they know that they belong to him.

While we may expend our effort trying to figure out who belongs and who doesn't, the Holy Spirit works to make us a single flock. The Spirit of God seeks to unite us under the one true Shepherd. St. Peter discovered that "God shows no partiality" (Acts 10:34b). God shows no partiality. That is because God gives each of us *all* of his love. None of us requires preferential treatment. We need not worry about being treated fairly, for each of us is uniquely favored. God sees us all as belonging to him, not one any more than another. That belonging is the deepest thing we share, and the loveliest gift we can give to one another.

Holy Spirit, Spirit of Oneness, you bring many together as one flock. Move to unite us in your love. Help us to

both give and accept the gift of belonging. Enable us to make our lives truly inclusive. Bridge every difference, every disparity, every distance between our hearts. Teach us patience with one another. Show us how to bend toward one another, to be more who we are because of one another. Help us to be fair to all our children. Keep us from partiality of any kind. Empower us to give all our love to each child. Gather us together as one family, sharing a common identity and life in you. Amen.

36

Tough Questions

What to Do When Your Child Asks

Nicodemus said to him, "How can anyone be born after having grown old? Can one enter a second time into the mother's womb and be born?" Jesus answered, "Very truly I tell you, no one can enter the kingdom of God without being born of water and Spirit. What is born of the flesh is flesh, and what is born of the Spirit is spirit. Do not be astonished that I said to you, 'You must be born from above.'"

— John 3:4–7

When anyone asks our two youngest daughters where they're from, one says "Russia," and the other says, "Mommy's tummy." (Not exactly the answers people expect!) While a great deal of literature has been dedicated to extolling the glories of Mother Russia, I'm not sure that the parallel really holds up. Listening to them, I can't help but think about apples and oranges.

Children have rather fragmentary understandings of their own origins. Our adoptive daughter, however, has a few more variables to fit into her equation than her other brothers and sisters. Trying to exercise her powers of logical thinking, Masha has come up with more than a few explanations about where she came from and how she got here. Because Masha doesn't remember having any family in Russia, she concluded at one point that she had mystically popped out of the orphanage walls. Her younger sister, on the other hand, envies Masha's exotic origins. Faraway and distant lands are, after all, far more interesting places to come from than your mother's innards. Next to Russia, Mommy is rather unattractive and anticlimactic.

Masha's confusion about past relationships has been evident in funny ways. About a year after she came home, I received an e-mail from a woman who had adopted a little girl from the same Voronezh orphanage that Masha came from. As it turned out, it was actually one of the little girls we had met along with Masha; Valentina had come home about a month after we had arrived with Masha. Masha was very excited to see Valentina's photo. After quite a round of jumping up and down, she promptly asked if Valentina was her sister!

While Masha has been less than certain about her origins, her younger sister seems to have it all figured out. Weaving a fantastic (and completely fictional) plot, she told me that Masha's family in Russia had died. With great compassion, she talked about how Masha had found her way on foot to the orphanage because she wanted a family. In her version, the baby house was a place where her sister's wish came true. All that the story was missing was the "once upon a time" at the beginning, and the "happily ever after" at the end. I wish it had all been that sweet.

Adoptive children have just as many questions as biological children. To us as parents, however, it may seem as though they have more questions simply because we have fewer answers. When our sons and daughters ask about where they came from, it is important that we go back beyond the time we first met them. It is not uncommon for adoptive children to think of themselves as never having been born. If the story we tell them starts somewhere in chapter two, it's easy to understand why they come to that conclusion. Every child comes into the world in the same way. Our adoptive children need to know that they are no different from anyone else in that respect.

The child of adoption has the great task of integrating two identities, and possibly even two very different lives. Parents can help their children do that by affirming the whole story. You need not provide more detail than is necessary, nor fill in missing information with conjecture. But when your child asks, you must tell the truth. Thankfully, it is possible to tell it in bite-sized, age-appropriate, and life-affirming pieces.

Children do not need the complicated terminology adults use to avoid making judgments. They should not, however, be made to feel that their own life histories are open to appraisal or criticism. While "single mother" could be confusing, "unwed mother" could make a child feel that he is somehow deficient. A better approach would be to tell the child that his birth mother was not married. While we might anticipate a series of follow-up questions, most children will take what they hear from us as an organic whole. Very few will analyze their stories bit by bit. A child takes his or her cue more from how we tell things than from what we have to say.

Adoptive parents should expect to answer the same set of questions again and again. Asking for the same information does not suggest that your son doesn't believe what you've told him; nor does returning to the same questions indicate that your daughter has rejected you in any way. As children grow in maturity, they will be able to absorb aspects of their personal histories differently. While our kids remember our every word, they need the reassurance that comes from hearing the tale repeated. Throughout your child's life, the same questions and answers will continue to hold something new for the journey toward self-discovery.

There are mysteries of origin and intimacy that we all find difficult to understand. The question Nicodemus poses to Jesus is as sincere as it is rhetorical. His question is not at all foreign to adoptive children and their parents. "How can anyone be born again? Is it possible for one to enter into his mother's womb a second time?" These questions are very real for the sons and daughters we adopt. They wonder, as do we, how it is that they might yet be "born" of us. The answer we may hear, if we are still, is that our families, while not born of flesh, are born of God's Holy Spirit. The longer we walk in that Spirit, the less astonished we will be that our lives must be born from above.

Jesus takes Nicodemus seriously and treats him sensitively. That is because our God takes questions. Whatever troubles us, whatever it is we long to know, God will hear and answer us. We may not completely understand what we hear. We may only be able to receive one small piece at a time. Nevertheless, our Father is ever attentive. Listening to the deepest questions of our hearts, the Holy Spirit witnesses the enduring power of new birth in each one of us.

Holy Spirit, Spirit of Revelation, you show us the truth in ways we can receive it. Help us to answer the questions our children ask with both honesty and love. Guide us

in revealing to them the stories of their lives in ways that affirm their lives as a whole. Show them that you have been present with them from the start, that you heard their needs and brought them home in love. Keep them from feeling guilt or responsibility for whatever happened to them. Protect them from anger. Lead them on the path of self-discovery. Help them to accept who they are and to become who you have created them to be. Amen.

37

A Language of Love
How We Talk About Adoption

> Yet the number of the people of Israel shall
> be like the sand of the sea, which can be
> neither measured nor numbered; and in the
> place where it was said to them, "You are not
> my people," it shall be said to them, "Children
> of the living God."
>
> — Hosea 1:10

Watching Masha acquire a new language was fasci-
nating. Before we even left Moscow, she had learned a
few English words, and her Russian had begun to lose
the luster of its native tones. While I hoped that she
would become bilingual, that just simply didn't happen.
Masha's understanding of English improved daily, but
her ability to speak in Russian declined right along
with it. There was one week in which Masha understood both languages, but couldn't really speak in

either one. That, I believe, was when she made her linguistic crossover. Afterward, Masha was an English-only child. For her, getting a new mother meant gaining a new mother tongue as well.

Masha was thrilled by her new life. One of the things she liked best was going on errands. That's why, when she started using the word "benka," I thought she meant "bank." While our daughter had little problem acquiring new vocabulary words, bank was inexplicably difficult for her to remember. For a few weeks, Masha kept talking about the benka and I kept correcting her pronunciation. Though it took me a while to notice, I finally figured out that most of what Masha was saying about this benka had nothing to do with banks. Putting the pieces together, it occurred to me that benka could be Russian babytalk for *dom rebyonka,* that is, "baby house." Masha hadn't meant bank at all. She had been talking about the orphanage all along.

Adoption adds new members to our families and new words to our personal lexicons. Not everyone we encounter, however, will speak the same language. The words people use reveal their inner dispositions and attitudes. This is particularly clear when the subject of conversation is adoption. If I had a quarter for every time someone asked me how much I knew about Masha's "real" mother, I would be a rich woman indeed. Usually, I let it go. But in my mind's eye I imagine telling them that they are looking at Masha's real mother and that I hadn't felt particularly fake when I got up that morning! Even more bothersome are those who—in front of our children—have the nerve to ask which kids are my "own." My impish self would love to inquire if they thought that I had kidnapped someone else's child or just picked one up while shopping. Bread, milk, someone else's child...these supermarkets really do have everything!

Other phrases are a lot subtler and, I think, insidious. After we had brought Masha home, I noticed that it was common to talk about birth as if it was something in the past. In contrast, adoption was always held in the present tense. "Juanita was born," but "Janine is adopted." Even stranger is the logic behind that use of language. It seems to make adoption and birth mutually exclusive. In common parlance, it is almost as if adoptive children were never born.

Adoptive families have the right to claim the language of adoption. The words we choose and those we use with our children will set the tone for those around us. How we talk about adoption—and whether we do—communicates more to our children than it does to others who may be listening. Positive and affirming language can help our kids feel more secure in who they are and how they came to us. Further, it is possible to gently correct those who, mostly unintentionally, use terms that may make an adoptive child feel less a part of his family than other children. As parents, we are responsible for educating people who have an ongoing presence in our children's lives. The words we've chosen to use should be shared with all our close friends and relatives. Universal language crusades, however, are neither necessary nor productive.

As children become ready to attend school, a whole new set of challenges arises. Classroom projects, especially those in the early grades, can present unforeseen difficulties for adoptive children. Some of our kids simply don't have baby photos that they can share with their classmates. Others, like our daughter, will never know what they weighed at birth. The concept of a "family tree" is far too narrow for children who enjoy relationships with both birth and adoptive family members. A simple and direct conversation with your child's teacher as soon as such assignments are given almost always solves any problems your child might have. I have found it helpful to share the essentials of our daughter's story with her teachers at the beginning of each school year. I've yet to encounter any who were unwilling to help by being a bit creative when it mattered.

Words change our perceptions of ourselves and of others. The language we use to express our experience of reality shapes how we experience that reality. Without contradicting what is objectively true, in a certain sense, we are what we are said to be. The trick lies in knowing just who is doing the saying!

The children of Israel became more numerous than the grains of sand on the shore; the people God chose had grown into a mighty nation. Yet, at a particular latitude and longitude in their history, they did not belong. At a place deserted and without hope—perhaps at a place in their hearts—they heard words that negated their very existence: "You are not my people." What desolation and abandonment they must have felt. With that breath they lost everything, not merely all they had, but all they were, all they had become.

Still, the people of Israel had been the people of God. With a second word, they could be that again. Just a word could bring them out from the shadows and into the light of the Holy One. The very same place of desolation could become a place of security and joy. God's word could make the difference. If the Almighty said to them, "Children of the Living God," that alone would make them so.

Through experience, Israel discovered that who they actually were depended completely on who God said they were. The divine word was truth. It still is. The heavenly Father claims each of us as children. We are adopted into the heavenly household by the very same power by which our adoptive children become ours; that is, by the power of words. Words are able to make us one because they are far stronger than anything that distinguishes us.

The language of the Holy Spirit is a lexicon of love. In God's grammar, we are always the object—the recipients—of his loving action. Every sentence is in the active voice. Every verb is in the present tense. There is no third person, no one outside the dialogue of belonging, for all our hearts belong to the Father who calls us his children. If only we could learn to speak God's language of love to ourselves and to one another!

Holy Spirit, Inspiration of the Word, give us the words we need to affirm our children. Help us to think and speak creatively, to find ways to express what you have done in our lives with gratitude and wonder. Keep us from words that hurt, that open up old wounds or threaten new injuries. Guide our interactions with others who are ignorant or insensitive. Show us how to share our lives with them in positive ways. Help us to speak love and commitment to one another, and to bring that language of love to all we meet. Amen.

38

Making You Mine

Adoption As a Lifelong Process

I am my beloved's and my beloved is mine.
— Song of Songs 6:3

*M*asha practiced saying the name we gave her, *Ma-ri-an-na Chris-tine*. She liked to enunciate every syllable distinctly, as if she was beating it out on a drum. Anyone who asked her what her name was got the long and drawn out formal answer. Nonetheless, Masha was still very much Masha. While we called her Maria too, the nickname suited her infinitely better.

About nine months after she first came home, Masha took command of the dinner table conversation. Waiting until everyone was listening (that can take a while), she began to make an announcement. "My name is Ma-ri-an-na Chris-tine Wolfe." Smiling at how cute she was, we all started to pick up where we had left off. Masha, however, wasn't finished. She continued, "Call me Ma-ri-an-na. I'm not Masha or Maria or those other names anymore." My eyes filled up with tears. I asked her if that was what she really wanted. "Ma-ri-an-na," she said, and with that, Masha disappeared.

I have always thought of that November supper as the day our daughter adopted us. No judge was present, no papers were necessary, and no translators were needed. Marianna had left her old life behind. She was ready—at that moment—to define herself in a new way, by a name that we had given her. Our daughter was truly ours not because we had a piece of paper that said she was, but because she had said so herself.

Up until that time, all the decisions that affected Marianna's life had been made by other people. Irina kept her birth a secret. A government official decided to place her in protective care. A Russian court deprived her birth mother of maternal rights. When Alla determined that she could not adopt her, she brought her into the room to meet us. We chose her. When a judge concurred, she got onto a plane with us and flew halfway around the world.

On that November evening, Marianna sensed that something had changed, that what she felt counted in ways it had never counted before. Marianna had become part of something greater than herself. She was one of us; she was ours and we were hers.

Adoption is not a court date. It is a lifelong practice of loving. The adoption process never ends, and even after we bring our children home, it is never truly complete. As we live more of our lives together as family, we continue to find new gaps to bridge and new ways of belonging to each other.

When I fill out the post-placement reports that are still required of us, I see how far Marianna has come. She is not the little girl we met in Voronezh. Marianna isn't afraid as she used to be. She doesn't move, or speak, or cry, or even eat the way she did when she first came to us. Our daughter does not act like an orphan, because she no longer is one. When we look at the photographs we took of her, she seems like a completely different child. The distance Marianna has traveled is much greater than the number of miles from Russia to the United States. She has crossed a great deal more than eight time zones. Marianna has found her way home. Still, our daughter's journey is nowhere near finished. In some ways, it has only just begun.

Our adventures, too, have barely gotten underway. There is so much ahead for us to become, both as individuals and as a family. As our children grow into adolescence and adulthood, our paths will undoubtedly twist and turn. There may be days when light is dim, and nights that make us question whether morning will ever come. But, through every darkness we encounter, we will shine in each other's lives. Like the North Star, our places are fixed in one another's hearts.

The Song of Songs is a duet sung by lovers. Longing for loving union, wanting to make her his own, the Lover calls his beloved forth. Unsure of where her Lover's intense passion may lead, she tarries in coming to him. While the desire of his heart is completely fixed on her, she flutters through the streets, seeking but not really finding what she is looking for. Longing to love, she does not experience the depths to which she is loved. In wanting the Lover to belong to her, she does not see herself as "beloved." She overlooks the sweetness of belonging to him.

Each one of us is the beloved of God. Many, however, do not feel the reality of the Father's love. Perhaps like the beloved, we are afraid or unnerved. Perhaps it is because we want to be the one to take the initiative. Whatever the reason, the end result is the same. We do not feel that we belong to God, or that he belongs to us.

Belonging is mutual, not individual. People become ours when we become theirs. The same holds true in our lives of faith. After all, the spiritual life is meant to be a love song. Our Father desires for us to belong to him and to one another. God is always seeking to make us his own. Taking us into his heart, the Holy Spirit waits for us to invite him into ours. The Lord so loves us that he gives himself completely into our hands. God does not make us his, that is, he does not force us to belong to him. Instead, the divine Lover makes himself ours. The Eternal One gifts himself to us.

When we adopt, we make a gift of our hearts and lives to a child. We do not know whether our sons and daughters will ever give themselves to us. Yet, like the Spirit who inspires us, we do it just the same. We choose to belong to our children in the hope that our children will someday belong to us.

God's love teaches us to give what we have received. Through living by faith every day, we belong more to God and become more like him. The purpose of our lives is to become God's completely. Knowing the Father's love for us the way our children know our love for them, we pass from belonging to belonging. At the end of our journey, when all is still, we will listen to the voices of those at heaven's table pronouncing the names by which they will be called. And as eternal day is dawning, we will hear the song of songs rise from the home that the Holy Spirit has made in our hearts. "I am my beloved's," we will sing, and the Lord will answer, "My beloved is mine!"

Holy Spirit, Spirit of Adoption, continue to lead us, not only in what we do, but in how we think, in how we decide, in how we see ourselves and others. Bring us to the

love that makes us truly yours. Help us to bear that same love to our children. May your fruit in our lives—love, joy, peace, patience, kindness, generosity, faithfulness, gentleness, and self-control—sustain our lives together. May your presence with us sweeten our days and fill our hearts. Teach us to give ourselves as you do: freely and totally as gift. Give us the grace to accept the gift of self that others—even our children—long to give us. Help us to hear your call throughout our lives and to answer it according to your will. Amen.

Appendix

Order for the Blessing of Parents and an Adopted Child

Introduction

302 The adoption of a child is an important event in the lives of a married couple or a single parent. This blessing serves as a public thanksgiving for the precious gift of a child and as a welcome of the child into its new family.

303 If the child is old enough to respond, provision is made for the child to accept the new parents as his or her own. In this case, the introduction of the rite should be adapted to the circumstances, and a more appropriate reading may be chosen.

304 If there is only one parent, the rite should be adapted to the circumstances by the minister.

305 This order may be used by a priest or a deacon, and also by a layperson, who follows the rites and prayers designated for a lay minister.

ORDER OF BLESSING

Introductory Rites

306 When the community has gathered, a suitable song may be sung. After the singing, the minister says:

In the name of the Father, and of the Son, and of the Holy Spirit.

All make the sign of the cross and reply:

Amen.

307 A minister who is a priest or deacon greets those present in the following or other suitable words, taken mainly from sacred Scripture.

May the love of God be with you always.

And all reply:

And also with you.

---

308 A lay minister greets those present in the following words:

Let us praise our loving God.

Blessed be God for ever.

R. Blessed be God for ever.

---

309 In the following or similar words, the minister prepares those present for the blessing.

It has pleased God our heavenly Father to answer the earnest prayers of N. and N. for the gift of a child. Today we join them in offering heartfelt thanks for the joyful and solemn responsibility which becomes theirs by the arrival of N. into their family.

Reading of the Word of God

310 A reader, another person present, or the minister reads a text of sacred Scripture.

Brothers and sisters, listen to the words of the holy gospel according to Mark: 10:13–16

Jesus blesses the little children.

People were bringing children to Jesus that he might touch them, but the disciples rebuked the people. When Jesus saw this he became indignant and said to the disciples, "Let the children come to me; do not prevent them, for the kingdom of God belongs to such as these. Amen, I say to you, whoever does not accept the kingdom of God like a child will not enter it." Then he embraced the children and blessed them, placing his hands on them.

Or:

Deuteronomy 6:4–7—Diligently teach your children.

Deuteronomy 31:12-13—Do this that your children may hear.

1 Samuel 1:9-11, 20-28; 2:26—The birth and presentation of Samuel.

Matthew 18:1-4—Those who humble themselves like children will be the greatest.

Luke 2:22-32, 52—Presentation of Jesus in the temple.

As circumstances suggest, one of the following responsorial psalms may be sung; or some other suitable song.

R. O LORD, our God, how wonderful your name in all the earth!

O LORD, our Lord,
how glorious is your name over all the earth!
You have exalted your majesty above the
    heavens.
Out of the mouths of babes and sucklings
you have fashioned praise because of your
    foes,
to silence the hostile and the vengeful. *R.*

When I behold your heavens, the work of
    your fingers,
the moon and the stars which you set in
    place—
What is man that you should be mindful of
    him,

or the son of man that you should care for
    him? *R.*

You have made him little less than the
    angels,
and crowned him with glory and honor.
You have given him rule over the works of
    your hands,
putting all things under his feet. *R.*

All sheep and oxen,
yes, and the beasts of the field,
The birds of the air, the fishes of the sea,
and whatever swims the paths of the seas. *R.*

O LORD, our Lord,
how glorious is your name over all the earth!
    R.

Psalm 78:1–7

*R. (v. 4) Tell the coming generations the glorious deeds
of the Lord.*

As circumstances suggest, the minister may give
those present a brief explanation of the biblical
text, so that they may understand through faith the
meaning of the celebration.

Acknowledgment by the Child and Parents

The minister asks the parents:

You have received N. into your family;
will you (continue to) love and care for him/her?

Parents:

We will.

If the child is old enough to answer, the minister asks:

You have accepted N. and N. as your parents; will you love and respect them?

The child replies:

I will.

The minister says:

As God has made us all his children by grace and adoption, may this family always abide in his love.

The *Canticle of Mary* or another hymn of praise may then be sung.

Intercessions

The intercessions are then said. The minister introduces them and an assisting minister or one of those present announces the intentions. From the following those best suited to the occasion may be used or adapted, or other intentions that apply to the particular circumstances may be composed.

The minister says:

God is the author of all life and calls us into his loving family; with thankful hearts we pray:

R. Loving Father, hear us.

Assisting minister:

For the Church throughout the world, that it may nurture, guide, protect and love all who are joined to it in baptism, let us pray to the Lord. *R.*

Assisting minister:

For N. and N. and their new son/daughter, N., that God may bind them together in love as a family in Christ, let us pray to the Lord. *R.*

Assisting minister:

[For the brother(s) and sister(s) of N., that they may grow in friendship and love, let us pray to the Lord. *R.* **]**

Assisting minister:

For married couples who desire the gift of a child, that God may hear their prayers, let us pray to the Lord. *R.*

Assisting minister:

For all Christian families, that the love of Christ may dwell in their homes, let us pray to the Lord. *R.*

After the intercessions the minister, in the following or similar words, invites all present to sing or say the Lord's Prayer.

As God's children by adoption, we pray:

All:

Our Father...

Prayer of Blessing

A minister who is a priest or deacon says the prayer of blessing with hands outstretched over the parents and child; a lay minister says the prayer with hands joined.

Loving God,
your Son has taught us
that whoever welcomes a child in his name,
    welcomes him.
We give you thanks for N.,
whom N. and N. have welcomed into their
    family.
Bless this family.
Confirm a lively sense of your presence with
    them
and grant to these parents patience and wis-
    dom,
that their lives may show forth the love of
    Christ
as they bring N. up to love all that is good.

We ask this through Christ our Lord.

R. Amen.

As circumstances suggest, the minister in silence may sprinkle the family with holy water.

Concluding Rite

A minister who is a priest or deacon concludes the
rite by saying:

**May almighty God, who has called us into
the family of Christ,
fill you with grace and peace,
now and forever.**

R. Amen.

Then he blesses all present.

**And may almighty God bless you all,
The Father, and the Son,+ and the Holy
Spirit.**

R. Amen.

A lay minister concludes the rite by signing himself or
herself with the sign of the cross and saying:

**May almighty God, who has called us into the
family of Christ, fill us with grace and peace,
now and for ever.**

R. Amen.

It is preferable to end the celebration with a suitable
song.

BOOKS & MEDIA

The Daughters of St. Paul operate book and media centers at the following addresses. Visit, call or write the one nearest you today, or find us on the World Wide Web, www.pauline.org

CALIFORNIA

3908 Sepulveda Blvd, Culver City, CA 90230	310-397-8676
5945 Balboa Avenue, San Diego, CA 92111	858-565-9181
46 Geary Street, San Francisco, CA 94108	415-781-5180

FLORIDA

145 S.W. 107th Avenue, Miami, FL 33174	305-559-6715

HAWAII

1143 Bishop Street, Honolulu, HI 96813	808-521-2731
Neighbor Islands call:	800-259-8463

ILLINOIS

172 North Michigan Avenue, Chicago, IL 60601	312-346-4228

LOUISIANA

4403 Veterans Memorial Blvd, Metairie, LA 70006	504-887-7631

MASSACHUSETTS

885 Providence Hwy, Dedham, MA 02026	781-326-5385

MISSOURI

9804 Watson Road, St. Louis, MO 63126	314-965-3512

NEW JERSEY

561 U.S. Route 1, Wick Plaza, Edison, NJ 08817	732-572-1200

NEW YORK

150 East 52nd Street, New York, NY 10022	212-754-1110
78 Fort Place, Staten Island, NY 10301	718-447-5071

PENNSYLVANIA

9171-A Roosevelt Blvd, Philadelphia, PA 19114	215-676-9494

SOUTH CAROLINA

243 King Street, Charleston, SC 29401	843-577-0175

TENNESSEE

4811 Poplar Avenue, Memphis, TN 38117	901-761-2987

TEXAS

114 Main Plaza, San Antonio, TX 78205	210-224-8101

VIRGINIA

1025 King Street, Alexandria, VA 22314	703-549-3806

CANADA

3022 Dufferin Street, Toronto, ON M6B 3T5	416-781-9131

¡También somos su fuente para libros, videos y música en español!